Evolution of the Internet

37145

Series Editor: Cara Acred

Volume 230

Independence Educational Publishers

First published by Independence Educational Publishers

The Studio, High Green

Great Shelford

Cambridge CB22 5EG

England

© Independence 2012

Copyright

Photocopy licence

British Library Cataloguing in Publication Data
Evolution of the Internet. – (Issues ; v. 230)

1. Internet – Social aspects – Great Britain. 2. Internet – Safety measures.

I. Series II. Acred, Cara.

303.4'834-dc23

ISBN-13: 9781 86168 623 7

Printed in Great Britain
MWL Print Group Ltd

Contents

Introduction

Evolution of the Internet is Volume 230 in the *Issues* series. The aim of the series is to offer current, diverse information about important issues in our world, from a UK perspective.

ABOUT EVOLUTION OF THE INTERNET

30 million people in the UK go online on a daily basis; paying bills, shopping, watching films, chatting with friends and meeting new people. The Internet is an extremely powerful tool, but unfortunately it can also be a dangerous place for both adults and children. Internet safety is becoming a major issue for parents and schools, and there are increasing debates concerning our rights and privacy online. This book explores the evolution of the Internet, looking at how we live through technology and considering how we can take full advantage of the net, without compromising our safety.

OUR SOURCES

Titles in the *Issues* series are designed to function as educational resource books, providing a balanced overview of a specific subject.

The information in our books is comprised of facts, articles and opinions from many different sources, including:

- Newspaper reports and opinion pieces
- Website fact sheets
- Magazine and journal articles
- Statistics and surveys
- Government reports
- Literature from special interest groups

A NOTE ON CRITICAL EVALUATION

Because the information reprinted here is from a number of different sources, readers should bear in mind the origin of the text and whether the source is likely to have a particular bias when presenting information (or when conducting their research). It is hoped that, as you read about the many aspects of the issues explored in this book, you will critically evaluate the information presented.

It is important that you decide whether you are being presented with facts or opinions. Does the writer give a biased or unbiased report? If an opinion is being expressed, do you agree with the writer? Is there potential bias to the 'facts' or statistics behind an article?

ASSIGNMENTS

In the back of this book, you will find a selection of assignments designed to help you engage with the articles you have been reading and to explore your own opinions. Some tasks will take longer than others and there is a mixture of design, writing and research based activities that you can complete alone or in a group.

FURTHER RESEARCH

At the end of each article we have listed its source and a website that you can visit if you would like to conduct your own research. Please remember to critically evaluate any sources that you consult and consider whether the information you are viewing is accurate and unbiased.

Digital Britain

The truth about how we live today through technology.

Half the country go online every day

There are 62 million people in the UK[1] and more of us are going online, and spending more time there, every day.

By August 2011, 77% of households[2] were connected (up 4 percentage points on 2010), with 30 million going online every day or almost every day. 93% of them have broadband connections of 2Mbps or higher[3], nearly a quarter (24%) had 10Mbps or above[4] and 1% clocked in above 24Mbps in May 2010[5]. In other words, a sizeable chunk of the country has access to the Internet and data-heavy services like advanced websites and video.

We're internationally mediocre for coverage and speed

However, globally, that's poor: we dawdle at 26th on broadband penetration and speed rankings, with Bradford the unlikely and only British city to enter the global top 100. Generally, the south and cities are much better catered for than the north and countryside. The Government knows this – and knows how closely coupled high-speed Internet is with improving the economic and social prospects of British homes and businesses.

More Internet in more places coming

To that end, UK Culture Minister Jeremy Hunt has committed to get Britain the best superfast broadband infrastructure in Europe by the end of the current parliament and is investing £830 million against this[6]. If that pans out, a pretty decent network is only going to get better, paving the way for more powerful and rich Internet experiences.

Mobile, the new kid on the block

While most of us still go online at a desk, mobile is increasingly dragging us away. In 2009 23% went online with a phone. By 2010 it was 31%. In 2011 it was 45%[7]. To restate: nearly half of all Internet users are doing it on their phones. Nor is it the case that these people are dusting off an old WAP device and checking their email. By 2012 46% of Brits were using a smartphone[8], a growth on the previous year so deep in double digits it's not even worth stating as it will be out of date in a month.

It's likely this rate of growth will remain, or even ramp, in the coming years as smartphones go mainstream and the infrastructure gets a makeover with a new network, called the 4G mobile spectrum, landing in 2013.

This will offer a big improvement on the current 3G network, which is limited to around 3.6Mbps, by allowing for speeds of up to 100Mbps out and about, or ten times that (1Gbps) when stationary, to around 95% of the country. That means while a one-minute YouTube video would take 30 seconds to download on today's mobile network, an HD feature length film would take about a tenth of the time on 4G. In other words mobiles will no longer have to pull data through the keyhole: the door will be wide open.

This will usher in a blazingly fast mobile experience. In this world, the majority of the processing will happen in vast servers and all anyone's mobile has to do is reach up into this 'cloud computer' and tap into it, unconstrained by download speeds. Phones tomorrow will do what today's best desktops can, just quicker.

Digital Britain is established and only going to get more established, in speed, geography and devices.

But what are people actually doing online?

The traditional Internet

The great time vampire

We spend around 57 hours per month on computers[9]. Roughly half that time is spent offline in Word and PowerPoint, organising photos, watching films and playing games. The rest is spent online.

So central is the Internet to people's lives that a third of Brits claim they couldn't live without it[10]. In fact, collectively we are living with it more every day. In 2009 the average time

1 Office of National Statistics (ONS)

2 Office of National Statistics (ONS) as cited by eMarketer, September 2011

3 Office of National Statistics (ONS) as cited by eMarketer, September 2011

4 Trends in broadband supply and uptake http://www.scotland.gov.uk/Publications/2011/02/23091236/9

5 Ofcom, as quotes on BBC http://www.bbc.co.uk/news/technology-11922424

6 Telegraph, http://www.telegraph.co.uk/technology/broadband/8448680/Superfast-broadband-scheme-proposed-for-5-million-rural-homes.html

7 http://www.ons.gov.uk/ons/publications/re-reference-tables.html?edition=tcm%3A77-226727

8 http://paidcontent.org/article/419-smartphone-penetration-approaching-tipping-point-as-pc-usage-declines-/ 3

9 UKOM: http://www.thedrum.co.uk/news/2011/04/28/21101-overview-of-uk-online-measurement-data-for-march-2011/

spent online per day was 41 minutes; within a year it had jumped 20% to 52 minutes[11]; by the start of 2012 it was 1 hour 12 minutes, or 36 hours a month[12]. Mobile Internet access will drive this stat into the absurd and we'll soon be online more than we're awake. It will be like saying how long an average person has access to oxygen for in a day.

What are people doing online?

If a man were to sit down at his computer, send a few emails, hunt for some information, research and buy some stuff, check his bank balance, pop onto Facebook while listening to some music he downloaded, then game for a while before discussing it on a forum and finish up the day telling a mate on Skype how he sold something on eBay for a hefty profit, he would pretty much have exactly summed up British online activity – in decreasing order of frequency.

Here's a more thorough breakdown:

Although average time online and frequency is instructive in the broad sense, it's a 'white rainbow', a bland average masking the colourful nuances.

Let's break it down, ladies first.

Women drive the digital mainstream

Globally, there are fewer women on the Internet than men, but they spend more time on it. In the UK, women have overtaken men online (51.3% vs 48.7%)[14] and reflect the broader pattern of heavier usage, spending about 8% more time online[15]. For UK housewives specifically, nearly half of all their leisure time is spent online[16].

Two major activities account for this.

The social sex

Globally, women spend 30% more time on social networks than men[17] – a figure that has held constant into late 2011 with European women clocking up 8.2 hours a month on social networks versus men who register at 6.3[18]. There are also more of them on social networks. In Europe 81% of men use social networks, trumped by women at 86%, a pattern that holds out for all regions. It's also good not to forget the less sexy but fundamentally central role of email and instant messaging, both activities where women talk men under the table on a global scale[19].

The shopper of the species

Globally, women spend 20% more time on retail sites than men[20]. Women buy more often than men, accounting for 59% of purchases on European websites (53% in the UK), but don't spend as much as men when they do. While European men spend 93.12 euros on an average web purchase, women spend 68.65 euros[21]. In the US, women buy more often than men too, but end up spending more. US women make up just under half of the Internet population but generate 58% of e-commerce dollars[22].

The traditional digital woman

Unsurprisingly, community, lifestyle and health sites – especially around parenting, food and home – continue to get more ladies dropping by than men[23]. British women are also nosier than their men, with 14% of wives reading their husband's emails and 10% checking their browsing history, (those figures for men are 8% and 7%, respectively[24].) Clearly, technology has neither got in the way of men's sexual proclivities nor the orbiting suspicions of women.

Women defy digital expectations

So far we've seen nothing a casual

bit of stereotyping wouldn't spit out. But there are some surprising findings which armchair bigots might not guess.

Game birds

Yes, cars, sport and a lot of high finance are still male-dominated but in personal finance and financial advice women have the edge, both in numbers visiting these sites and time spent on them.

In online gaming women are a level ahead too[25], although only on the gentler, casual games. Women overindex on puzzle, card, arcade, board, casino and trivia games while the genres of action, adventure and sports are typically favoured by young guys. Leading the charge in gaming for the girls are the over 45s who spend nearly a third more time than men their age playing[26].

Add a bit of spice to the major themes mentioned – being social and spending – and you get to some of the more surprising female pursuits online.

Bad girls

For example, porn slides in above the already-popular health, clothing and family and parenting sites in overall global usage for women. Some 34% of ladies admit to using adult sites, while for men it's 46%[27]. And given the obvious methodological problems of asking people whether they get their kicks from commoditised, choreographed human flesh, it's probably safe to give a Viagra to those percentages.

Other studies show British women are especially prurient. Six out of 10 women say they watch porn online[28] and an alarmingly high 17% of women describe themselves as 'addicted'[29].

Girls gamble

Gambling is pretty much a parity

10 GB TGI Net Q4 2009, December 2009

11 UKOM, December 2009

12 http://www.zdnet.co.uk/blogs/tech-tech-boom-10017860/brits-top-Internet-addicts-league-in-europe-10025436/ (36 hours divided by 30 days = 1.2 hours per day. 0.2 of an hour is 12 minutes.

13 Digital Trends Winter UK December 2011, Mintel

14 Estimated data from http://www.emarketer.com/Reports/All/Emarketer_2000391.aspx

15 ComScore, July 2010

16 http://news.bbc.co.uk/1/hi/technology/7789494.stm

17 ComScore - http://bit.ly/9dth6f

18 http://www.comscoredatamine.com/2011/12/women-spend-more-time-social-networking-than-men-worldwide/

19 ComScore - http://bit.ly/9dth6f 6

20 ComScore - http://bit.ly/9dth6f

21 http://www.Internetretailer.com/2011/03/28/european-women-shop-more-often-online-men-spend-more

22 ComScore - http://bit.ly/9dth6f

23 ComScore - http://bit.ly/9dth6f

24 http://www.networkworld.com/news/2010/052410-women-more-likely-to-snoop.html

25 ComScore - http://bit.ly/9dth6f

26 ComScore - http://bit.ly/9dth6f 7

27 ComScore - http://bit.ly/9dth6f

28 http://www.guardian.co.uk/culture/2011/apr/07/women-addicted-Internet-pornography

29 http://www.Internet-filter-review.toptenreviews.com/Internet-pornography-statistics-pg6.html

sport too. About 7% of adults fritter away their cash online and women are, in fact, more likely to visit some gambling sites than men (e.g. lotto and sweepstakes)[30].

Being geeky

Maybe most surprising is that global reach across all ages for technology sites doesn't vary that much between the sexes, although men spend more time there. Women may be geekier for less time but they're still being geeky[31].

Watching less

When it comes to online video, although reach is the same as men, women watch a lot less video, especially in the UK. Men spend nearly 20 hours a month watching, women barely reach ten hours[32]. One clue to what's going on here might be from the fact that women watch a lot more YouTube than men, as a share of their overall viewing. So while men are filling up on a fulsome show or film length video, women are snacking from YouTube.

Searching less

Women also search less than men[33]. One theory to explain this is that while men might be employing more of a direct, hunter-style strike to pin down information, women are using their 30% more time on social networks than men[34] to shortcut the searching process by asking friends first.

Dolls and dollars

With the exception of mobile (see later section), women are the backbone of the Internet: buying, chatting and playing, in innocent and not-so-innocent ways. To brands, the cleavage between social and spending should be attracting a lot of attention – therein lies enormous opportunity.

Digital blokes

Porn, tech and sport; that's all that needs to be said about men online, isn't it? Not quite. The picture is a little more nuanced. If women are nurturers – putting more time into maintaining social networks, searching less and getting information from their friends – men are the information and entertainment hunters.

Information, information, information

Finding, storing and writing information. That's what the men like to do. Men search more than women (71.6 searches per searcher per month for men vs 64 for women, US base[35]). When interacting with brands in social media, 36% of men claim information is their primary goal, while for women it's 28%[36]. They're also more likely to make use of browser bookmarking than to search again[37]. And finally, it's the men making Wikipedia. Barely 13% of Wikipedia's contributors are women[38].

Watching, learning, listening

In terms of entertainment, the most popular activities for British men online are watching video (51% vs 42% of women), visiting chat rooms/message boards/forums (32% vs 24% of women), listening to Internet radio (again, 32% vs 24% of women), listening to downloaded music (31% vs 22% of women) and downloading and playing games (14% vs 6% of women).

The chat room/message board/forum point is interesting: although women spend more time in social media overall, men outnumber them on this specific sector of social media, arguably because boards like this allow men to be much more specific in their information gathering.

Sport, cars and tech

Around 40% of the global online male population read about sport online[39,40], with women not far behind at around 35%. However, men are considerably more engaged spending nearly twice as much time on these sites[41].

When it comes to cars it's a similar but less marked story: between 25% and 35% of the online male population visit automotive sites (increasing with age) while women clock in between 20% to 30% and spent about 75% of the time men do on these sites[42].

Technology is different. Apart from a small male lead in reach at the younger ages, around 55-60% of the sexes go to technology websites, with women only spending about 10% less time there[43]. The common assumption that tech is for the boys is just not supported by the data.

Male preference for e-tail but overall still prefer a real shop

35% of men prefer 'e-tail' to real shops compared to 29% of women[44]. That's interesting because, although there is a slight male preference, most people prefer going to real shops. There are obvious reasons for this: you can touch and try in real shops – and they're a richer experience. Nevertheless, this preference suggests interesting user experiences that bridge the on- and offline worlds for both sexes.

What are they buying most?

Men may prefer to use online shopping more than women but they fall short of women on nearly all types of online shopping, only overindexing slightly on insurance and flights (they clearly like to get their oar in on the serious purchases) and, surprisingly, aligning on tech. A list of the most popular major online male purchases looks like this[45]:

⇨ 37% buy CDs or DVDs (women, 40%)

⇨ 32% go to eBay (women, 41%)

30 ComScore - http://bit.ly/9dth6f

31 ComScore - http://bit.ly/9dth6f

32 ComScore - http://bit.ly/9dth6f

33 ComScore - http://bit.ly/9dth6f

34 ComScore - http://bit.ly/9dth6f

35 ComScore - http://bit.ly/9dth6f

36 Empathetica, http://chiefmarketer.com/social/metrics/gender-difference-retail-social-media-011211/?cid=nl_cm_direct

37 Lightspeed Research 2009 http://www.iabuk.net/en/1/mensactivitiesonline.html

38 http://www.nytimes.com/2011/01/31/business/media/31link.html?_r=3&hp=&adxnnl=1&adxnnlx=1296491313-Gb/z5Xc+t9PSsze7krGSRg 9

39 ESPN 2009. Accessed from: http://www.iabuk.net/en/1/toptipsfortargettingmenonline.html in 2011; now no longer online

40 http://www.marketingcharts.com/direct/women-encroach-on-male-sites-13840/comscore-online-women-sports-sites-august-2010jpg/

41 ESPN 2009 Accessed from: http://www.iabuk.net/en/1/toptipsfortargettingmenonline.html in 2011; now no longer online

42 ComScore - http://bit.ly/9dth6f

43 ComScore - http://bit.ly/9dth6f

44 http://oxygen.mintel.com/sinatra/oxygen/search_results/show&&type=NSItem&class=News&sort=recent&display=abridged&page=1/display/id=574641&anchor=574641

45 Digital Trends UK, Spring, Mintel 10

46 Digital Trends UK, Spring, Mintel

- ⇨ 38% get clothing and footwear (women, 45%)
- ⇨ 30% buy books (women, 40%)
- ⇨ 22% kit up on toys and games (women, 28%)
- ⇨ 20% get insurance (women, 17%)
- ⇨ 20% book flights (women, 19%)
- ⇨ 19% buy tickets for entertainment, like gigs and theatre (women, 21%)
- ⇨ 17% buy music (women, 19%)
- ⇨ 18% buy gifts like flowers or confectionary (women, 26%)
- ⇨ 16% buy gadgets (women, 16% too)
- ⇨ 15% buy food online (women, 24%)

What are they buying least?

- ⇨ 13% get cosmetics and perfumes (women, 27%)
- ⇨ 13% purchase software (women, 10%)
- ⇨ 10% book holidays (women, 10% too)
- ⇨ 10% buy DIY and garden products (women, 9%)
- ⇨ 9% buy computer hardware (women, 5%)
- ⇨ 8% get home furnishings (women, 13%)
- ⇨ 8% buy mobiles (women, 8% too)
- ⇨ 5% purchase healthcare products (women, 10%)[46]

The connected child

For most of today's children the Internet is like air: it's just there and always has been. It's also everywhere: in the bedroom, in school, in their hands and even in their games console. However, there's still a wealth gap that needs to be closed before all children have Internet access.

Most online, most gaming

Over 90% of children have Internet access at home and the majority also use the Internet at school[47]. The average seven to ten-year-old now spends around eight hours a week online, climbing to 18 hours a week for 11-14s and 24 hours a week for those aged 15-19[48]. To repeat: teens are spending nearly half the time most people spend working per week just being online. What are they doing? As much as 70% claim that gaming is their most common online activity[49], equating to five million regular young gamers.

Poor kids left behind

While the breadth and depth of the Internet for Britain's young is astonishing, there is a sorry shortfall among the poor. In the richest 10% of homes, 97% had an Internet connection whereas in the poorest 10% of homes only 30% were connected[50]. The fear is that the technology gap is also breeding an attainment gap not just in computer literacy but also in all the attendant benefits being connected brings.

Growing up smart

Children are being brought up bathed in bits. Nearly half (41%) of 12 to 15-year-olds have Internet in their bedrooms, a leap of 31% in growth from 2009. Interestingly, nearly a quarter (23%) are going online via a games console. The phrase 'digital natives' isn't too far off.

It's perhaps time to give the phrase a younger cousin: the 'smartphone native'. Around 18% of five to 15-year-olds own a smartphone and 16% go online via a games console[51]. Among 12 to 15-year-olds this rises to 35% owning a smartphone[52].

To give that its context, smartphone penetration in the UK is estimated to be around 45% in 2012. In other words, the kids aren't far behind before they've even done their GCSEs.

Deep digital

And digital life is much more of their life. Rather heart-wrenchingly, 45% said they were sometimes happier online than in their real lives[53] and, while this could be that they just have more fun playing games online than sitting uninspired in a classroom or being told to finish their plates, it does point to the depth of relationship the coming generation has with the Internet. So strong is this relationship that among children aged 12-15, television is no longer the media most would miss were it to be taken away. Instead, 26% now say they'd most miss their mobile, while 24% say the Internet[54]. Half of children say they would be 'sad' and 10% saying they'd be 'lonely' if they didn't have an Internet connection[55].

What's interesting is that there are only a few percentage points in it: television still holds a very strong appeal. Anyone saying TV's dead for the younger generations shouldn't.

And we should be careful about following this fact into the future. Actual television viewing might decrease and the kids might say they'll miss it less if it's taken away but the amount of television content watched probably won't change; it will just be seen on different devices. It's the word television that's going to go out of fashion, not the shows on it.

Social from the start

Over half (54%) of children aged eight-15 who use the Internet at home have a social networking profile[56]. As for Facebook, 44% of eight to 13-year-olds are on it and 66% of six-year-olds are aware of it[57]. A quarter of children with a smartphone say that they regularly visit social networks on their phone[58].

Silver surfers

Catching up

Internet users over 65 are a relatively small group, accounting for only 6.1%

47 Youth TGI as cited by MediaTel, November 2010

48 Youth TGI as cited by MediaTel, November 2010

49 Survey commissioned by Disney as cited in "Next generation Media", Intelligence, Aegis Media, January 2010

50 http://www.guardian.co.uk/technology/2010/dec/28/uk-children-home-computer-access 11

51 http://consumers.ofcom.org.uk/2011/04/half-of-parents-know-less-about-the-Internet-than-their-children/

52 http://consumers.ofcom.org.uk/2011/04/half-of-parents-know-less-about-the-Internet-than-their-children/

53 http://www.kidscape.org.uk/events/saferInternetday2011.asp

54 http://consumers.ofcom.org.uk/2011/04/half-of-parents-know-less-about-the-Internet-than-their-children/

55 http://www.telegraph.co.uk/technology/news/9045134/British-children-feel-sad-without-Internet-connection.html 12

56 http://consumers.ofcom.org.uk/2011/04/half-of-parents-know-less-about-the-Internet-than-their-children/

57 http://www.thedrum.co.uk/news/2012/02/07/survey-find-larger-percentage-uk-children-using-facebook-us

58 http://consumers.ofcom.org.uk/2011/04/half-of-parents-know-less-about-the-Internet-than-their-children/

59 UKOM: http://www.thedrum.co.uk/news/2011/04/28/21101-overview-of-uk-online-measurement-data-for-march-2011/

of the UK online audience in March 2011[59]. That said, they're the fastest growing age bracket. In 2010 in the UK around 35% of over 65s had broadband[60].

The poor

A bit behind

If you breakdown the Internet population by socio-economic group there is a robust pattern: poorer people have poorer Internet penetration. The good news is that the less affluent are catching up fast at 13.4% since 2009[62], a slowing down on the previous rate most readily explained by the recession and increased vigilance over discretionary spend.

Interaction with advertising

Click deflation

Between 2004 and 2009 click-through rates on online adverts fell precipitously to 0.07%. Now, only one ad in 1,500 is clicked[63,64].

Retargeting

However, all is not lost in online advertising. Have you ever seen an ad online that reminds you of something you were doing a few days ago on a site? That's because when you went to that site it dropped something called a cookie onto your machine. That cookie was just a record of what you looked at. The ad you got served was uncannily related to the stuff you were looking at because your computer is telling it what you were looking at. This is retargeting and it is enjoying triple the normal click-through rate of online ads at about 0.22%[66]. However, there is an even more effective type of online advertising.

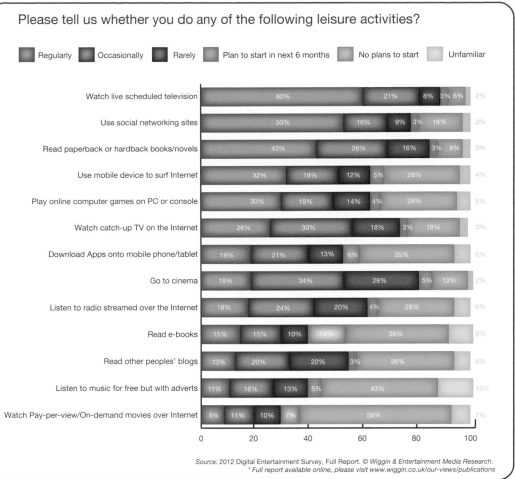

Please tell us whether you do any of the following leisure activities?

Source: 2012 Digital Entertainment Survey, Full Report. © Wiggin & Entertainment Media Research.
* Full report available online, please visit www.wiggin.co.uk/our-views/publications

Contextual targeting

Ever been on a site and seen an ad that seems to be on exactly the same subject as the page you're on? This is contextual targeting and is six times more effective than the industry average, enjoying 0.45% click-through rates[67]. And contextual targeting is cheaper. In fact, you get five times the clicks as retargeting at around half the price[68].

Summary

In short, the Internet is getting wider, flatter and deeper. More people are getting it. The demographic differences are being ironed out. And we're spending more time on it from childhood right through to old age. That said, there are important differences in usage, from women's social and spending habits to men's information and entertainment addiction to children's increasing Internet and mobile immersion. The way people interact with advertising is changing too: we are no longer as interested in the general, the personalised and contextual grab us – a lesson many brands simply don't yet know.

⇨ The above information is reprinted with kind permission from DARE. Please visit www.thisisdare.com for further information on this and other subjects.

© 2012 DARE

---

60 GB TGI Kantar Media UK Ltd Q1 2005-2011 (Oct – Sept) Mintel 13

61 Researching Purchases Online – UK April 2011, Mintel

62 Kantar as cited by MediaTel, June 2010

63 Forrester and DoubleClick, cited here https://docs.google.com/present/view?id=d5sr9zx_1625hdsh9gfj&pli=1

64 Mad Men are watching you http://www.economist.com/node/18651104 14

65 Forrester and DoubleClick, cited here https://docs.google.com/present/view?id=d5sr9zx_1625hdsh9gfj&pli=1

66 Forrester and DoubleClick, cited here https://docs.google.com/present/view?id=d5sr9zx_1625hdsh9gfj&pli=1

67 Forrester and DoubleClick, cited here https://docs.google.com/present/view?id=d5sr9zx_1625hdsh9gfj&pli=1

68 Forrester and DoubleClick, cited here https://docs.google.com/present/view?id=d5sr9zx_1625hdsh9gfj&pli=1

Digital divide risks becoming a gulf

Latest research from the Communications Consumer Panel into digital participation.

The Internet seems to be all around us and it's easy to assume everybody uses it. Yet the stark fact is that about 11 million people in the UK do not use the Internet at home.

The latest research from the Communications Consumer Panel warns that there is a serious risk that public policy is underestimating the challenge of supporting people to get online and stay online. Panel Chair Jo Connell explains how its 2012 report *Bridging the gap: sustaining online engagement* explores people's digital needs, perceptions and experiences, and recommends actions to support more people online.

Bridging the gap highlights that while there is a drive for public and commercial services to be online, just over one in five UK adults (22%) in the UK still do not use the Internet at home. In some areas around the UK this percentage is far higher, for example, as it is in the most deprived areas of Glasgow. This means that a significant minority of people risk being excluded from online benefits and services – a situation that will only get worse as access to more and more services becomes Internet based.

The research identifies key barriers that create resistance to people using the Internet, and drivers that encourage them towards it. Consumers who took part in the research said:

Lapsed user (someone who has tried the Internet but stopped using it and not gone back), female 70s: 'I like going down to the post office. It gets me out and about and meeting people. I don't want to stay indoors and stare at a computer screen.'

Proxy user (unable or unwilling to use the Internet themselves, and who rely on someone else to go online for them), male 50s: 'I know you can get cheaper car insurance online. But I prefer the phone, so I get my son to find some good quotes for me and then I ring them up.'

Narrow user (someone who has gone online but uses the Internet very little), female 20s: 'You know, by the time you've got the computer turned on and up and running, I could have done it all on the phone in half the time.'

New user (people who have largely overcome initial perceived barriers and are developing confidence and new skills online), female 60s: 'I sit and press the buttons and keep pressing them until it works.'

The report follows on from the Panel's earlier work into the importance of Internet use. The 2009 research *Not online, not included: consumers say broadband essential for all* found: the majority of consumers (81% agreed) considered that it was everyone's right to be able to have broadband at home, regardless of where people lived; and that it should be possible for people to gain the confidence and skills to make full use of broadband at home (80% agreed). It noted that there was a tipping point... when broadband does not just provide an advantage to people who have it, but disadvantages people who do not...

Jo Connell says that the 2009 report rightly envisaged a future where more services are delivered solely online or provided offline in a way that penalises people who do not have broadband at home: 'This reduces their options and opportunities and makes them pay more.'

The Panel's 2010 *Framework for digital participation* is also playing a key role in supporting people to get online. Jo Connell explains: 'The Framework reflects people's views about what they need at each stage of their digital participation journey, and I'm delighted that a number of organisations, including the RNIB (Royal National Institute of Blind People), are using the Panel's five-stage approach.'

The 2012 *Bridging the gap* research has clear implications for future funding, growth and policy – as the distance increases between online consumers and people who remain anchored in the offline world. Jo Connell says that she is pleased that Ofcom has now accepted the Panel's recommendation to include mobile coverage obligations for each of the nations in the forthcoming spectrum auction: 'This is a significant opportunity to increase Internet access by bringing mobile broadband to at least 98% of people.'

Jo Connell says that clear targets are now needed to assess the progress being made in supporting people to get and stay online, including action to give people the skills to exploit the advantages of the Internet – or there is a risk the digital divide risk will become a digital gulf: 'The Panel wants to see the Government strike a better balance between funding for broadband infrastructure and supporting people online. Sustainable growth for the future can only be achieved if broadband is used by most consumers and businesses.'

References:

⇨ *Bridging the Gap: Sustaining online engagement:* http://www.communicationsconsumerpanel.org.uk/smartweb/research/bridging-the-gap:-sustaining-online-engagement

⇨ The Consumer Panel's *Framework for digital participation:* http://www.communicationsconsumerpanel.org.uk/smartweb/digital-participation/the-consumer-framework-for-digital-participation

⇨ *Not online, not included: consumers say broadband essential for all:* http://www.communicationsconsumerpanel.org.uk/downloads/not%20online%20-%20not%20included%20-%20June%202009.pdf

⇨ Communications market research: http://stakeholders.ofcom.org.uk/market-data-research/market-data/communications-market-reports/cmr12/

⇨ The above information is from the Communications Comsumer Panel. Please visit www.communicationsconsumerpanel.org.uk.

© Communications Consumer Panel 2012

The broadband debate: need for speed?

Information from the International Telecommunication Union.

There is a wealth of recent evidence suggesting that the Internet can contribute significantly to the economy, economic growth, job creation, and innovation in the development of new services and applications. For example, a 2011 analysis of 13 countries by the McKinsey Global Institute found that the Internet contributed 11 per cent of growth over the past five years. This important topic is examined in a report by the Broadband Commission for Digital Development, 'Broadband: A Platform for Progress', published in June 2011 (see June 2011 issue of *ITU News*).

The range and quality of services that can be offered over the Internet is greatly enhanced by faster data rates. High-speed infrastructure is surely a win-win situation – good for consumers, who enjoy greater choice of services; good for governments and national competitiveness in their communications infrastructure and ability to attract foreign direct investment and create jobs in diverse sectors; and good for industry, where operators sell faster Internet connectivity to gain competitive edge and market share at higher prices and, potentially, higher margins (witness the 4G wars, for example).

But how fast is fast enough? And what factors need to be taken into account in setting targets for speed and deploying infrastructure? Speed does not always mean reliability – and the relationship between speed and reliability is not always easy.

ITU News and the Broadband Commission for Digital Development are launching a new series of mini-debates to promote the objectives of the Commission, underlining the importance of broadband infrastructure in helping accelerate progress towards achieving the Millennium Development Goals. This first debate examines the need for speed.

Slow, but steady?

Sometimes, it is basic connectivity that matters, regardless of the speed of the connection. The phenomenal growth of 2G mobile connectivity in the developing world has done much to empower the previously unconnected, whether by giving people livelihoods (for example, the Grameen 'phone ladies' of Sri Lanka and Uganda) or simply by making people contactable and more available for work.

In the developing world, lack of infrastructure often prevents health workers from delivering health care efficiently to isolated patients in rural areas. Some of the gaps in local health systems can be mitigated using simple, locally appropriate communication technologies. In Malawi, Medic Mobile has used SMS and mobile open-source platforms (including Ushahidi, Google Apps and HealthMap) to mobilise communities for vaccination campaigns, collect data and map health services. Using text messages and mobile phones, St. Gabriel's Hospital in Malawi has tracked new symptoms and doubled the number of patients being treated for tuberculosis, while saving thousands of hours of travel and work time. Medic Mobile is using mobile technology to great effect to monitor drug stocks in rural Ethiopia, track vaccinations in India, support the prevention of mother-to-child transmission of HIV in Malawi and streamline test result delivery for cervical cancer screening in Nicaragua.

In agriculture, e-Krishok is an initiative launched by the Bangladesh Institute of ICT in Development in Bangladesh, which aims to provide farmers with both general information and answers to specific questions through a web-portal. This project has grown from just ten locations in October 2008 to 100 centres with Internet and mobile access by February 2010, as e-Krishok has become the preferred source of information for the many farmers reached by the campaign.

These real-life examples show how even basic ICT can make a real difference to the way people live, work or get health care. Part of the success of these projects is attributable to the use of robust technologies and simple devices that are reliable and do not need a lot of power.

Faster is automatically better?

If these are the gains that can be achieved through low-speed applications, imagine how much more could be achieved through high-speed connections. Although a precise definition of broadband is elusive (speed of upload versus download, and whether this capacity is sustained in data transfer rates to the exchange or end user), broadband as a concept embraces high-speed, high-capacity, always-on access to ICT services capable of providing various services (voice, video and data).

ITU recognises fixed (wired) broadband services as subscriptions to high-speed access to the public Internet (over a TCP/ IP connection) at downstream speeds equal to, or greater than, 256 kbit/s. Booz & Company note, for example, that speeds of up to 100 Mbit/s are needed for some telemedicine and distance learning applications, compared to 4–6 Mbit/s required for web-based teleconferencing.

The Phoenix Center in the United States sees the true value of broadband access to a society as varying according to its use, connection speed and method of access. Some countries (such as Denmark) have set national targets for achieving specified levels of coverage with certain speeds by set dates. France and the European Union are seeking to provide universal coverage of broadband Internet access. The UK's Digital Britain Plan envisages 100 per cent coverage of rural areas with 2 Mbit/s service, in part as the minimum speed needed to deliver iPlayer, the BBC's Internet TV service, although this target has been deemed modest by some observers. Other countries are now including broadband Internet in their definitions of universal service.

National targets for coverage and transmission capacity (speed) are an important signal by governments of their commitment to establishing the foundations for a modern economy with advanced infrastructure.

Fast enough?

In order for broadband to thrive, and for the market to grow successfully, national targets and operators' deployment plans should take account of customer needs and the geography of the areas, as well as what the technology is likely to be used for. How fast is fast enough depends on these, more specific, factors.

In an era where data usage is growing at an explosive rate, sometimes at a cost to quality of service, operators have to deploy technologies to meet the needs of specific markets or specific geographies in certain areas (for example, urban versus rural), according to the distribution of customers – for example, Clearwire's selection of new markets for the deployment of mobile broadband in certain areas of the United States. A mismatch between speed and usage may mean that consumers in developing countries find that technologies are not locally appropriate to their real needs. Consumers in developed countries are already finding that brakes are being applied to their data capacities – both for fixed as well as mobile service. In the United States, AT&T has set limits on customers' use of its high-speed network (with charges for additional capacity), and similar arrangements are common in Canada, Asia and Europe. Matching speeds to needs seems to be the way to go.

⇨ Reprinted from ITU News, Issue No. 7, September 2011, published by the International Telecommunication Union. Please visit www.itunews.itu.int/en/ for further information on this and other subjects.

The Net Generation, unplugged

Is it really helpful to talk about a new generation of 'digital natives' who have grown up with the Internet?

They are variously known as the Net Generation, Millennials, Generation Y or Digital Natives. But whatever you call this group of young people – roughly, those born between 1980 and 2000 – there is a widespread consensus among educators, marketers and policymakers that digital technologies have given rise to a new generation of students, consumers and citizens who see the world in a different way. Growing up with the Internet, it is argued, has transformed their approach to education, work and politics.

'Unlike those of us a shade older, this new generation didn't have to relearn anything to live lives of digital immersion. They learned in digital the first time around,' declare John Palfrey and Urs Gasser of the Berkman Centre at Harvard Law School in their 2008 book, *Born Digital*, one of many recent tomes about digital natives. The authors argue that young people like to use new, digital ways to express themselves: shooting a YouTube video where their parents would have written an essay, for instance.

Anecdotes like this are used to back calls for education systems to be transformed in order to cater to these computer-savvy students, who differ fundamentally from earlier generations of students: professors should move their class discussions to Facebook, for example, where digital natives feel more comfortable. 'Our students have changed radically.

'Today's students are no longer the people our educational system was designed to teach,' argues Marc Prensky in his book *Digital Natives, Digital Immigrants*, published in 2001. Management gurus, meanwhile, have weighed in to explain how employers should cope with this new generation's preference for collaborative working rather than traditional command-and-control, and their need for constant feedback about themselves.

But does it really make sense to generalise about a whole generation in this way? Not everyone thinks it does. 'This is essentially a wrong-headed argument that assumes that our kids have some special path to the witchcraft of "digital awareness" and that they understand something that we, teachers, don't – and we have to catch up with them,' says Siva Vaidhyanathan, who teaches media studies at the University of Virginia.

Michael Wesch, who pioneered the use of new media in his cultural anthropology classes at Kansas State University, is also sceptical, saying that many of his incoming students have only a superficial familiarity with the digital tools that they use regularly, especially when it comes to the tools' social and political potential. Only a small fraction of students may count as true digital natives, in other words. The rest are no better or worse at using technology than the rest of the population.

Writing in the *British Journal of Education Technology* in 2008, a group of academics led by Sue Bennett of the University of Wollongong set out to debunk the whole idea of digital natives, arguing that there may be 'as much variation within the digital native generation as between the generations'. They caution that the idea of a new generation that learns in a different way might actually be counterproductive in education, because such sweeping generalisations 'fail to recognise cognitive differences in young people of different ages, and variation within age groups'. The young do not really have different

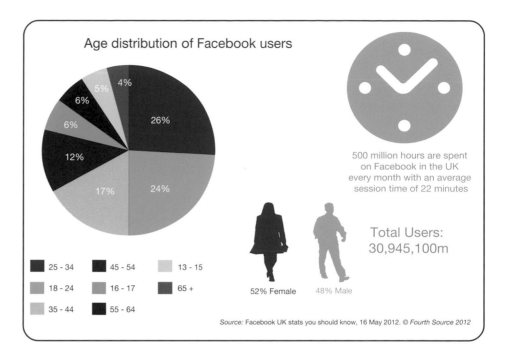

Age distribution of Facebook users

- 25 - 34
- 18 - 24
- 35 - 44
- 45 - 54
- 16 - 17
- 55 - 64
- 13 - 15
- 65 +

26% 24% 17% 12% 6% 6% 5% 4%

500 million hours are spent on Facebook in the UK every month with an average session time of 22 minutes

Total Users: 30,945,100m

52% Female   48% Male

Source: Facebook UK stats you should know, 16 May 2012. © *Fourth Source 2012*

kinds of brains that require new approaches to school and work, in short.

What about politics, and the idea that, thanks to the Internet, digital natives will grow up to be more responsible citizens, using their technological expertise to campaign on social issues and exercise closer scrutiny over their governments? Examples abound, from Barack Obama's online campaign to activism on Twitter. A three-year study by the MacArthur Foundation found that spending time online is 'essential for young people to pick up the social and technical skills they need to be competent citizens in the digital age'. But discussions about 'digital citizens' run into the same problems as those about digital natives: there may simply be too much economic, geographic, and demographic disparity within this group to make meaningful generalisations.

After all, not everyone born between 1980 and 2000 has access to digital technology: many in the developing world do not. It is true that the Internet can provide an outlet for political expression for people living under repressive regimes. But those regimes are also likely to monitor the Internet closely. And in some cases there is, in effect, a new social contract: do what you like online, as long as you steer clear of politics. Government-controlled Internet-access providers in

Belarus, for example, provide servers full of pirated material to keep their customers happy.

Activism or slacktivism?

There is also a feeling of superficiality about much online youth activism. Any teenager can choose to join a Facebook group supporting the opposition in Iran or the liberation of Tibet, but such engagement is likely to be shallow. A recent study by the Pew Research Center, an American think-tank, found that Internet users aged 18–24 were the least likely of all age groups to email a public official or make an online political donation. But when it came to using the web to share political news or join political causes on social networks, they were far ahead of everyone else. Rather than genuinely being more politically engaged, they may simply wish to broadcast their activism to their peers. As with the idea that digital natives learn and work in new ways, there may be less going on here than meets the eye.

4 March 2010

⇨ The above information is reprinted with kind permission from the *The Economist Newspaper* limited. Please visit www.economist.com for further information on this and other subjects.

Truth, lies and the Internet

A report into young people's digital fluency.

The Internet is now almost certainly the greatest source of information for people living in the UK today. We use it to read up on what is happening in the world, to get advice about things that worry us, to argue and collaborate, to decide who to vote for and who to date. The information we access and consume on the Internet is central to forming our attitudes, our beliefs, our views about the world around us and ours sense of who we are within it.

The amount of information available to us at the click of a mouse when making these decisions can be both liberating and asphyxiating. Although there are more e-books, trustworthy journalism, niche expertise and accurate facts and figures at our fingertips than ever before, there are equally unprecedented amounts of mistakes, half-truths, mis-truths, propaganda, misinformation, disinformation and general nonsense.

Making sense of all this – knowing how to discriminate the good, reliable, trustworthy or useful information from the bad – is therefore of tremendous importance. The ability to make these difficult judgements matters to everyone but especially young people, for whom the Internet is a more important medium than any other group.

Our research shows, however, that many young people are not careful, discerning users of the Internet. They are unable to find the information they are looking for or trust the first thing they do. They do not apply fact checks to the information they find. They are unable to recognise bias and propaganda and will not go to a varied number of sources. As a result, they are too often influenced by information they should probably discard. This makes them vulnerable to the pitfalls and rabbit holes of ignorance, falsehoods, cons and scams. Inaccurate content, online misinformation and conspiracy theories (such as those which surrounded the death of Osama bin Laden) are appearing in the classroom.

The potential consequences of this on society as a whole are unknown. One danger is that young people are more likely to be seduced by extremist and violent ideas. As we have argued elsewhere, many terrorist groups are fed by bogus online material circulating unchallenged on online echo chambers. Anders Breivik, the recent Oslo terrorist, is a devastating but only the most recent example of the power of Internet material to radicalise.

The answer is not greater censorship or a tighter control over Internet content. The task is to ensure that young people can make careful, sceptical and savvy judgements about the Internet content they will, inevitably, encounter. This would allow them to better identify outright lies, scams, hoaxes, selective half-truths and mistakes, and better navigate the murkier and greyer waters of argument and opinion.

The ability to judge the merits of different pieces of information is not new; it is the basis of much classical philosophy. However, the architecture and functionality of the Internet makes the job of separating the wheat from the chaff even harder. A specific body of skills and knowledge is required to make informed judgements. We use the term 'digital fluency' to describe this competence: the ability to find and critically evaluate online information. It is a combination of 'old' critical thinking skills, such as source verification, and 'new' knowledge about how the digital world works, such as understanding search engines. These are the bedrock skills necessary for the individual to use the Internet to search, retrieve, contextualise, analyse, visualise and synthesise information effectively.

We undertook two new pieces of research to determine the extent of digital fluency among young people in the UK. First, we reviewed current literature relating to digital fluency, including 17 surveys and other research papers, studies and reports undertaken between 2005 and 2010. Second, we conducted a survey of 509 teachers in England and Wales about the extent of their pupils' digital fluency.

Findings, literature review

Our literature review revealed that 'digital natives' (12–18 year-olds) are very confident users of the Internet, but are not particularly competent. There is some evidence to show that some young people are discerning, careful Internet users, but much else that indicates that the skills of digital natives do not match their own self-reportage:

Too many digital natives do not apply checks on the information they access

Around one in four 12–15-year-olds make no checks at all when visiting a new website, and less than one in ten ask who made the site and why.

Aesthetics over quality

Decisions about information quality is based on site design, rather than more accurate checks – around one-third of 12–15-year-olds believe that if a search engine lists information then it must be truthful; and 15 per cent don't consider the veracity of results but just visit the sites they 'like the look of'.

Lack of teaching:

Only one-third of 9–19 year olds have been taught how to judge the reliability of online information. 55 per cent of teachers surveyed in 2008 felt their students 'did not have sufficient understanding of what plagiarism was and what counts as legitimate research'.

Findings, Demos survey

Between 16 May and 16 July 2011, Demos conducted an online survey of primary and secondary school teachers in England and Wales about their views on their pupils' digital fluency, and how it might be taught in school. In total, we received 509 responses. This is the largest survey of its kind ever conducted.

The intention of the survey was to evince general attitudes within the teaching profession towards several themes:

⇨ the importance of the Internet and digital fluency skills;

⇨ the extent of their pupils' current digital fluency;

⇨ and the state of digital fluency within the school.

To this end, a sample with a reasonable spread of teachers (by seniority, subject and class-age) and schools (by geographical locale, school-type and sector), rather than a completely representative profile of all teachers and schools, was required. The results of the survey are therefore not perfectly representative of the teaching profession as a whole.

The online survey methodology and publication strategy we employed did not allow for a totally representative series of distributions and proportions within the sample cohort. However, we did apply post-stratification weightings (according to subjects taught, as measured by the School Workforce Census) to improve representativeness.

The findings include:

Internet teaching and learning is fundamental to pupils' school and personal lives:

88 per cent of teachers surveyed consider Internet-based research to be important for their pupils' schoolwork; and 95 per cent report that their pupils have brought information into the classroom they have found online. 75 per cent believe that Internet-based content to be important in the formation and validation of their pupils' beliefs.

Teachers are worried about their pupils' digital skills

99 per cent of teachers surveyed think that digital fluency is an important skill for pupils to possess, but across a range of measures, teachers rate their pupils' digital fluency skills as below average. In particular, the application of fact-checks or other source verification on the online information they consume, the ability to recognise bias or propaganda, and the variety of sites they visit, are rated most poorly.

Misinformation, propaganda, and conspiracy theories are being brought into the classroom

47 per cent of teachers surveyed report having encountered arguments within lessons or submitted schoolwork that contain inaccurate Internet-based content they regard as deliberately packaged by the producers to be misleading or deceitful (for example, holocaust denial packaged as radical historical revisionism). 18 per cent report this happens on at least a monthly basis. Perhaps more surprisingly, 48 per cent of teachers surveyed report having had arguments in class with pupils about conspiracy theories. More than one in five reported this happening on a monthly basis.

Teachers believe overwhelmingly that digital fluency needs to be given more prominence in the classroom

99 per cent of teachers surveyed consider digital fluency to be an important skill for young people to possess; and 88 per cent think it should be given more prominence in the national curriculum. Combining our survey results with the background literature review, we believe information literacy teaching in schools is struggling to keep pace with the rise of the Internet. The Internet has become central to learning, but the skills to use it appropriately and well have not become central to learning how to learn.

Recommendations

We recommend a major campaign to place digital

fluency at the heart of learning. In a context where young people are confronted with such a vast array of information, having the skills and knowledge to evaluate and assess that information is a fundamental skill that all children must possess. The Government, schools, Internet companies and providers, creative agencies, libraries and parents all have a role to play.

Digital judgment must become a core part of the National Curriculum and teacher training. The Government should include digital fluency as a 'core competency' in the National Curriculum during its current review. Digital fluency is a foundational, core skill that should underlie teaching and learning across all subjects, and is not confined to a single subject. As a minimum, all schools must teach pupils about search engines, propaganda techniques, source attribution techniques, and the risks of data-sharing. Although there are some promising initiatives in some schools, coverage is patchy and too many schools do not teach it. Given that an increasing number of schools will be operating outside the National Curriculum, this is something that academies and free schools should also take on themselves. The Department for Education must also ensure that these skills are taught as part of teacher training programmes.

'Misinformation often thrives because it is more attractively packaged'

The Department for Education should join forces with the private sector and third sector to create a set of teacher resources. The majority of teachers we surveyed were happy to teach digital judgement, but many said they need the materials, support and training to do so. Some teachers may lack confidence in relation to their use of ICT and do not always have the time to rectify it. Both the Department for Education and Internet companies such as Google and Yahoo! should create materials that can be used in the classroom, and where possible, teaching assistance. A bespoke web presence should be created to provide an overarching context for digital fluency teaching, organising the links, materials, lesson plans and examples necessary for classroom teaching.

Misinformation often thrives because it is more attractively packaged and disseminated as sharable, social media-friendly products. Teaching resources must use the same techniques to teach as young people use: YouTube videos, webinars, interactive tasks and podcasts. Moreover, Internet-borne misinformation often thrives on anti-establishment kudos, as a way for young people to assert independence of mind. A digital fluency campaign must not overly identify with authority, and should also include material that provides the opportunity

to critique and discuss establishment (be it official, government or school) decisions or actions.

Parents need to take a more active role in managing and guiding their children's online consumption, and encourage critical thinking. A decade ago, most children first encountered technology at school – now it is in the home. This is a dramatic change, because Internet use at home is relatively unsupervised for young people: over half of 12–15-year-olds say they 'mostly use the Internet alone', and 41 per cent of parents of this age group say that their child has access to the Internet in their bedroom, a rise from 31 per cent in 2009. Many parents think that the digital world is alien to them – a mysterious place inhabited by their 'digital native' children. They should not. Offline knowledge and critical thinking skills possessed by parents are of enormous relevance in an online setting, too. Parents need to be part of any campaign, and should start by becoming more familiar and confident with various aspects of Internet functionality as part of their child's general education, and imparting the importance of careful, thoughtful evaluation of information, whatever the source.

29 September 2011

⇨ The above information is reprinted with kind permission from Demos. Please visit www.demos. co.uk for further information.

© 2011 Demos

The changing face of digital literacy in UK schools and universities

Information from Metia.

By Lizzie Donnachie

Earlier this month saw Michael Gove, the UK's Education Secretary, propose new plans to scrap the existing ICT curriculum, allowing schools to design and tailor their own course. *The Guardian* helped spark reform throughout the week with its Digital Literacy Campaign.

Supported by blue chip companies such as Google and Microsoft, the aim was to improve the teaching of computing science and ICT through raising awareness of the disparity between the skills of UK students learned from their current curriculum and what the industry experts suggest is required for the economy. The UK Culture Minister – Ed Vaizey – has now ranked computer skills alongside the arts and humanities, 'we are all going to live a digital life... Just as we write well and read well... a basic understanding of computer coding will help you understand the structure of your digital life'.

'These digital skills contribute to the British economy'

Not only do these digital skills contribute to the British economy, it has also become in vogue among the younger generation with an increase in apps and a self-taught attitude to coding with websites and forums offering step-by-step tutorials. Therefore, as the digital economy expands, why has the UK education system not caught up and raised the importance of digital literacy within our classrooms?

There has been a dramatic decrease in the number of students opting to study ICT, what's more, girls are especially disinterested with the traditional 'geeky' image surrounding the subject. There has also been increasing case studies where students are becoming frustrated with the lack of resources invested in the ICT curriculum and unchanging syllabus, highlighting a drastic need to shake up the system.

Steve Beswick, Director of Education for the UK at Microsoft agrees and states that, 'we must introduce computer science concepts a lot earlier and this will help broaden the number of people that want to do this as a profession'.

The UK ICT education system is falling behind other countries such as South Korea, Israel and even Scotland – who are considered to be pioneers of teaching ICT. In Scotland, children as young as six start learning about the basics of computer science and schools strive to incorporate computing into almost every subject on the curriculum. In Uruguay, their 'one laptop per pupil' programme has proven successful and has helped to generate interest in the subject.

So what happens now for the future of digital literacy in the UK? Since Gove's new DIY-style reform, there is still a lot of uncertainty within the teaching of computer science in school. However, it does give schools and teachers the opportunity to listen to students and experiment with their syllabus to meet their student's and the economy's ever-changing needs.

Some interesting areas which *The Guardian* campaign revealed that schools should consider when designing their new syllabus are:

⇨ Reshaping the image perception of ICT for male and female students.

⇨ To widen the students experience of computing to more than PCs and Macs, but to experience other operating systems also.

⇨ Take advantage of the vast amount of material online and encourage self-teaching.

⇨ Relinquishing the control over teachers using social media within the classroom.

⇨ Technological innovations that could revolutionise classroom learning for the more complex subjects such as Maths, Design, Art and Science, including: gamification, programming, motion capture and animation modelling.

If nothing else this DIY-style reform should at least allow more forward thinking, technically competent teachers to develop best practices that can then be rolled out on a wider basis.

From a partner perspective it also opens up a number of potential opportunities for those channel players in the education sector to work with schools and universities to provide them with the technology they need. For example, the Rent-a-PC scheme Stone announced at BETT (British Educational Training and Technology Show) earlier this month.

23 January 2012

⇨ The above information is reprinted with kind permission from Metia. Please visit www.metia.com for further information on this and other subjects.

© 2012 Metia

Addicted! Scientists show how Internet dependency alters the human brain

***Information from* The Independent.**

By Jeremy Laurance

Internet addiction has for the first time been linked with changes in the brain similar to those seen in people addicted to alcohol, cocaine and cannabis. In a groundbreaking study, researchers used MRI scanners to reveal abnormalities in the brains of adolescents who spent many hours on the Internet, to the detriment of their social and personal lives. The finding could throw light on other behavioural problems and lead to the development of new approaches to treatment, researchers said.

An estimated five to ten per cent of Internet users are thought to be addicted – meaning they are unable to control their use. The majority are games players who become so absorbed in the activity they go without food or drink for long periods and their education, work and relationships suffer.

Henrietta Bowden Jones, consultant psychiatrist at Imperial College, London, who runs Britain's only NHS clinic for Internet addicts and problem gamblers, said: 'The majority of people we see with serious Internet addiction are gamers – people who spend long hours in roles in various games that cause them to disregard their obligations. I have seen people who stopped attending university lectures, failed their degrees or their marriages broke down because they were unable to emotionally connect with anything outside the game.'

Although most of the population was spending longer online, that was not evidence of addiction, she said. 'It is different. We are doing it because modern life requires us to link up over the Net in regard to jobs, professional and social connections – but not in an obsessive way. When someone comes to you and says they did not sleep last night because they spent 14 hours playing games, and it was the same the previous night, and they tried to stop but they couldn't – you know they have a problem. It does tend to be the gaming that catches people out.'

Researchers in China scanned the brains of 17 adolescents diagnosed with 'Internet addiction disorder' who had been referred to the Shanghai Mental Health Centre, and compared the results with scans from 16 of their peers.

The results showed impairment of white matter fibres in the brain connecting regions involved in emotional processing, attention, decision making and cognitive control. Similar changes to the white matter have been observed in other forms of addiction to substances such as alcohol and cocaine.

'The findings suggest that white matter integrity may serve as a potential new treatment target in Internet addiction disorder,' they say in the online journal *Public Library of Science One*. The authors acknowledge that they cannot tell whether the brain changes are the cause or the consequence of the Internet addiction. It could be that young people with the brain changes observed are more prone to becoming addicted.

Professor Michael Farrell, director of the National Drug and Alcohol Research Centre, University of New South Wales, Australia, said: 'The limitations [of this study] are that it is not controlled, and it's possible that illicit drugs, alcohol or other caffeine-based stimulants might account for the changes. The specificity of "Internet addiction disorder" is also questionable.'

Case studies: caught in the web

Xbox addict killed by blood clot after 12-hour sessions

Chris Staniforth, 20, died of a blood clot after spending up to 12 hours at a time playing on his Xbox. Despite having no history of ill health, he developed deep vein thrombosis – commonly associated with long-haul flight passengers. Mr Staniforth, from Sheffield, had been offered a place to study game design at the University of Leicester. But he collapsed while telling a friend he'd been having pains in his chest.

Toddler starved to death while mother played online

A mother was jailed for 25 years after her daughter starved to death while she played an online game for hours at a time. Rebecca Colleen Christie, 28, from New Mexico in the US, played the fantasy game World of Warcraft while her three-year-old daughter, Brandi, starved. The toddler weighed just 23lbs when she was finally rushed to hospital after her mother found her limp and unconscious.

Woman jailed after gamble fails to pay off

A woman who stole £76,000 from a company to fund her Internet gambling addiction was jailed this week. Lucienne Mainey, 41, from Cambridgeshire, was sentenced to 16 months in prison at Ipswich Crown Court after admitting fraud. The court heard she secretly paid herself by changing old invoices. Mainey turned to Internet bingo following the breakdown of her marriage.

12 January 2012

⇨ The above information originally appeared in *The Independent*. Please visit www.independent.co.uk for further information.

© *The Independent*

New research about Facebook addiction

Are you a social media enthusiast or simply a Facebook addict? Researchers from Norway have developed a new instrument to measure Facebook addiction, the Bergen Facebook Addiction Scale.

By Sverre Ole Drønen

The use of Facebook has increased rapidly. We are dealing with a subdivision of Internet addiction connected to social media, Doctor of Psychology Cecilie Schou Andreassen says about the study, which is the first of its kind worldwide.

Andreassen heads the research project 'Facebook Addiction' at the University of Bergen (UiB). An article about the results has just been published in the renowned journal *Psychological Reports*. She has clear views as to why some people develop Facebook dependency.

It occurs more regularly among younger than older users. We have also found that people who are anxious and socially insecure use Facebook more than those with lower scores on those traits, probably because those who are anxious find it easier to communicate via social media than face-to-face, Andreassen says.

People who are organised and more ambitious tend to be less at risk from Facebook addiction. They will often use social media as an integral part of work and networking.

Our research also indicates that women are more at risk of developing Facebook addiction, probably due to the social nature of Facebook, Andreassen says.

According to Andreassen, the research also shows that Facebook addiction was related to extraversion. People with high scores on the new scale further tend to have a somewhat delayed sleep-wake rhythm.

Six warning signs

As Facebook has become as ubiquitous as television in our everyday lives, it is becoming increasingly difficult for many people to know if they are addicted to social media. Andreassen's study shows that the symptoms of Facebook addiction resemble those of drug addiction, alcohol addiction and chemical substance addiction.

The Bergen Facebook Addiction Scale is based on six basic criteria, where all items are scored on the following scale: (1) Very rarely, (2) Rarely, (3) Sometimes, (4) Often and (5) Very often:

⇨ You spend a lot of time thinking about Facebook or plan use of Facebook.

⇨ You feel an urge to use Facebook more and more.

⇨ You use Facebook in order to forget about personal problems.

⇨ You have tried to cut down on the use of Facebook without success.

⇨ You become restless or troubled if you are prohibited from using Facebook.

⇨ You use Facebook so much that it has had a negative impact on your job/studies.

Andreassen's study shows that scoring of 'often' or 'very often' on at least four of the six items may suggest that you are addicted to Facebook.

About the scale

In January 2011, 423 students – 227 women and 196 men – participated in tests for the Bergen Facebook Addiction Scale. The scale can facilitate treatment research, clinical assessment and can be used for the estimation of Facebook addiction prevalence in the general population worldwide.

The Bergen Facebook Addiction Scale has been developed at the Faculty of Psychology, University of Bergen in collaboration with the Bergen Clinics Foundation, Norway. The researchers involved are also working with instruments measuring other addictions, such as the recently introduced Bergen Work Addiction Scale.

7 May 2012

⇨ The above information is reprinted with kind permission from the University of Bergen. www.uib.no

Internet addiction: the next new fad diagnosis

Article from The Huffington Post.

By Allen Frances

'Internet addiction' may soon spread like wildfire. All the elements favouring the fad generation are in place: the profusion of alarming books, the breathless articles in magazines and newspapers, extensive TV exposure, ubiquitous blogs, the springing up of unproven treatment programs, the availability of millions of potential patients, and an exuberant trumpeting by newly minted 'thought-leading' researchers and clinicians.

So far, DSM 5 has provided the only restraint. Exercising uncharacteristically wise decision making, it has chosen to rain on this parade by relegating Internet addiction to an obscure appendix rather than legitimising it as an official psychiatric diagnosis. But Internet addiction seems to be picking up steam even without DSM 5 endorsement.

There is no doubt that most of us have become hooked on our electronic devices, and that some people are gravely harmed by what develops into an unhealthy and uncontrollable attachment to them. The question is how best to understand, define and deal with this. What does the term 'addiction' mean, and when is it a useful way of describing our passions and needs? We don't consider ourselves addicted to our cars, TVs, refrigerators or air conditioners. Is attachment to the Internet fundamentally different? If so, how and what do we do about it?

The definition of Internet addiction is closely related to the definition of drug addiction, so this is the best place to start if we are to gain understanding and avoid confusion. Three features define drug addiction:

⇨ Tolerance: needing more to get the same kick.

⇨ Withdrawal: feeling terrible when you try to stop.

⇨ A pattern of compulsive use: continuing the substance even if the pleasure is largely gone and the cost is extremely high (e.g. terrible health, work, interpersonal, financial and/or legal consequences).

Drug addiction means being enslaved – not being able to stop using, despite the lousy cost/benefit ratio of no longer getting much pleasure from the drug while suffering much harm from it. This has to be clearly distinguished from the much more common pattern of recreational use (i.e., taking drugs because they are fun and accepting the harms because, at least in the short run, they seem worth it). Recreational use may lead to really stupid choices and dreadful outcomes, but it is not to be considered a mental disorder.

DSM 5 proposes to introduce a category of 'behavioural addictions,' with gambling as the first member and Internet addiction standing next in line to become a possible second. Behavioural

addictions could easily expand to eventually include passionate attachments to many other common activities. If we can be addicted to gambling and the Internet, why not also include addictions to shopping, exercise, sex, work, golf, sunbathing, model railroading, you name it? All passionate interests are at risk for redefinition as mental disorders.

The whole concept of behavioural addictions is highly controversial and has never heretofore been given any official status. There is a good reason for this. It is extremely difficult to distinguish the relatively few people who are really enslaved by shopping, sex, work, golf or the Internet from the huge army of those who are attached to these as pleasurable recreation. It should not be counted as a mental disorder and be called an 'addiction' just because you really love an activity, get a lot of pleasure from it and spend a lot of time doing it. To be considered 'addicted,' you should be compulsively stuck doing something that is no longer fun, feels out of control, serves no useful purpose, and is certainly not worth the pain, costs and harms. The unfavourable cost/benefit ratio should be pretty lopsided before mental disorder is considered.

We all do dumb things that offer short-term pleasures but cause bad long-term consequences. It is not 'addiction' whenever someone gets into trouble because of overspending, golfing too much or having repeated sexual indiscretions. That's our human nature, derived from many millions of years of evolutionary experience during a time when life was short, opportunities for pleasure rare and the long term didn't count for nearly as much as it does now. There is a risky slippery slope if we medicalise our pleasure-seeking, irresponsible selves. 'Addiction' could easily become an Oprah ready excuse for impulsive and irresponsible pleasure seeking ('I am really sorry I did it, but it is not my fault – my addiction made me do it!').

This brings us to 'Internet addiction.' Granted, lots of us are furtively checking emails in movie theatres and in the middle of the night, feel lost when temporarily separated from our electronic friends and spend every spare minute surfing, texting or playing games. But does this really qualify us as addicts? No, not usually, not unless our attachment is compulsive and without reward or utility; interferes with participation and success in real life; and causes significant distress or impairment. For most people, the tie to the Internet, however powerful and consuming, brings much more pleasure or productivity than pain and impairment. This is more love affair and/or tool using than enslavement and is not best considered the stuff of mental disorder. It would be silly to define as psychiatric illness behaviour that has now become so much a necessary part of everyone's daily life and work.

The best analogy is caffeine. Many millions of people can't get through the day without their treasured cups of coffee. Starbucks built its franchise and skillfully sited its drug distribution centres on the proven premise that coffee is addicting. In preparing DSM-IV, we excluded caffeine as an addictive substance only because it doesn't cause that much trouble for most of the people hooked on it. It seemed crazy to diagnose mental illness in all those people patiently waiting in line for their next hit. Most Internet users deserve equally benign neglect from psychiatric diagnosis. Ditto passionate shoppers, workaholics, sexual athletes, golfing fiends and dedicated sun worshipers. If the activity works for them, it is not to be labelled addiction and is not a mental disorder.

But what about the small minority of Internet users who really are stuck in a pattern of joyless, compulsive, worthless and self-destructive use – the 24/7 gamers, the shut-ins, the people trapped in virtual lives? The concept of addiction may indeed apply to many of them, and diagnosis and treatment may someday be proven to be useful, but not yet; it is still far too early to tell. We don't know how to define Internet addiction in a way that will not also mislabel the many who are doing just fine being chained to their electronics. We also don't know what proportion of excessive users are stuck on the Internet because they have a primary psychiatric problem that needs to be addressed first and may be missed if 'Internet addiction' becomes an explain-all, masking their underlying problems.

So far, the research on 'Internet addiction' is remarkably thin and not very informative. Don't get too excited by pretty pictures showing the same parts of the brain lighting up during Internet use and drug use; they light up non-specifically for any highly valued activity and are not indicative of pathology. The history of psychiatry is filled with fad diagnoses that far overshoot their target, get wildly misapplied and spawn new 'treatments' that are often no more than expensive quackery. 'Internet addiction' needs to be less a media darling and more a target of sober research.

South Korea is the most wired country in the world and has the biggest problem with excessive Internet use. The government is attempting to tackle this head-on with education, research and intelligent public policy, none of which has required declaring 'Internet addiction' a mental disorder. This is an excellent model for the rest of the world to follow. Deal with the problem of excessive Internet use as it exists in those who have it, without prematurely jumping to a label that may be misleading and is likely to unleash a set of harmful unintended consequences.

Despite all the media hype, it is way too premature to conclude that the Internet is controlling our lives, ruining our brains, and driving us crazy. We are not all Internet addicts. Let's stop this fad before it starts.

13 August 2012

⇨ The above information is from *The Huffington Post* and is reprinted with kind permission from AOL (UK) Limited. Please visit www.huffingtonpost.co.uk for further information.

© 2012 AOL (UK) Limited

Hooked on the Net?

Information from **Bang!** *Science Magazine.*

By Matthew Warren

The topic of Internet addiction is one which is sure to crop up, in some sensationalised form, every few months in the science section of newspapers. So it was not surprising to read this piece a few days ago in *The Independent*, reporting the results of a study by Lin and colleagues. The study found that the integrity of white matter (the brain tissue through which signals are transmitted) was reduced in the 17 subjects diagnosed with 'Internet Addiction Disorder'. These apparently 'groundbreaking' results show just how serious Internet addiction can be. Putting aside any issues with interpretation of the original study itself (we all know that correlation does not equal causation!), what is common to all of these kinds of articles is the unquestioning – and perhaps mistaken – acceptance of Internet Addiction Disorder as a real mental illness.

'The mental health professional's Bible, does not currently recognise addiction per se as a mental disorder'

The Diagnostic and Statistical Manual of Mental Disorders (DSM), the mental health professional's Bible, does not currently recognise addiction per se as a mental disorder. Thus, early researchers compared symptoms of substance dependence (or drug addiction, which is in the DSM) with those of excessive Internet users. They found that Internet addicts often appeared to fit the criteria, which included 'heavier use than intended' and 'large time devoted to use'. Particularly influential was Dr Kimberley Young. She attempted to create a formal definition of Internet addiction by adapting the DSM criteria for another disorder called pathological gambling. This led to the development of the Internet Addiction Test, a version of which was used in the study reported by *The Independent*, and which is available online here at Young's website.

Studies using such tests have found that 5–10% of respondents fit the criteria for 'addiction', and some have called for Internet Addiction Disorder to be recognised in the next version of the DSM. However, defining Internet addiction based on criteria for substance dependence or pathological gambling seems fundamentally flawed. While gambling or taking drugs are essentially unconstructive behaviours, Internet use incorporates a variety of activities, many of which are productive. Indeed, Internet use may often allow us to perform 'normal' tasks through a different medium. If this is the case, should we even be concerned if our use appears excessive? Have a look at Young's Internet Addiction Test, but imagine that 'on-line' and 'Internet'

were substituted with 'hanging out with friends'. I'm sure that many of us often 'hang out with friends longer than intended' or 'fear that life without friends would be boring', but we would find it ridiculous if someone suggested that we had 'Friend Addiction Disorder'. Yet, socialising is one of the major activities associated with the Internet. Similar logic can be applied to other Internet-enabled activities such as reading, watching TV shows or educating ourselves.

The idea of people suffering from some general Internet addiction thus seems too simplistic. Indeed, what appears to be Internet addiction may often be addiction to a certain aspect of the Internet, which could still manifest itself in the absence of the web. For example, someone who is addicted to Internet gambling probably suffers from pathological gambling rather than addiction to the Internet. Apparent compulsive use of the Internet may also be symptomatic of some other underlying disorder. In a 2000 paper, Shapira and colleagues found that 20 subjects displaying 'problematic Internet use' all fit the criteria for other disorders as well, the most common being mood and anxiety disorders. Other studies have found similar results. To illustrate this point, consider someone with social anxiety, who may use the Internet a lot because they are scared to go out. If the Internet did not exist, then they may equally have stayed home watching TV excessively.

'The idea of people suffering from some general Internet addiction thus seems too simplistic'

Ironically, the term 'Internet Addiction Disorder' was first coined by Dr Ivan Goldberg as a joke. It served as a protest against the tendency toward seeing behaviours as medical conditions. It seems fitting to give him the last word:

'To medicalise every behaviour by putting it into psychiatric nomenclature is ridiculous. If you expand the concept of addiction to include everything people can overdo, then you must talk about people being addicted to books, addicted to jogging, addicted to other people.'

20 January 2012

⇨ The above information is reprinted with kind permission from *Bang!* Science Magazine and Oxford Student Publications Limited. Please visit www.bangscience.org for further information.

Getting the elderly online – improving quality of life

Let's be honest, apart from mobility aids we tend to assume the elderly and technology don't make for a good mix. We think they're unwilling to embrace new things and come from a generation which struggles with programming the video.

We'd be wrong. Facebook an elderly-free zone? Definitely not – over-65s are the fastest growing age group there. Online dating a younger person's game? Think again – over-50s are joining Match.com faster than any other age group.

Society is slowly waking up to the fact that the Internet is a place which can benefit everyone and that the elderly are using it more than ever.

It's no wonder, since this is the generation which has most to gain. Many parents bemoan the fact their kids spend too much time online and ought to be outside playing and being active. For the elderly, opportunities for going out can become more restricted, making the benefits to be had from surfing much greater. So it's time for the young to start bemoaning the fact their elderly parents aren't spending time online! Indeed, you should do everything you can to make that happen!

The benefits of senior surfing

When you stop to think, suddenly it becomes clear just how vast the potential is for improving the quality of your elderly parents' lives with the Internet.

Isolation

This is the most obvious benefit. The Internet is designed to connect people and if you're increasingly housebound it can be a great way to interact with others and simply feel part of society again. The elderly can participate in online book groups, find old friends in social networks or join sites related to their past, such as war veterans groups. It also helps them keep close to relatives who may be far away. Grandchildren who live on another continent can now be seen on a Skype call whilst photos and videos can be shared in an instant.

Shopping

One of the things the elderly find most frustrating is not being able to shop so easily. Mobility can make trailing round shops a problem, struggling with bags is an effort and if they no longer drive even getting to the shops in the first place can be a trial. Shopping on the Internet is advertised as convenient for younger people so just think how much more true that is for the elderly.

Stimulation

There is endless variety on the Net and as limitations start to narrow your parents' lives, the web can open them up again. Beyond news, entertainment sites and even games, there's the potential for exploration. One elderly gentleman gained huge satisfaction finding online photos of the ships he sailed on during the war whilst others have enjoyed using Google maps to revisit childhood haunts. All of this stimulation brings positive benefits for mental health.

Empowerment

One of the most depressing aspects of growing old is the sense of losing power. The Internet can help restore this, not only through the feeling of having more access to the world but also through the possibilities for communication. On discussion boards the elderly can have a voice that's heard and they are also able to contact MPs and people in authority with much greater ease.

Improving offline life

The resources available online can provide endless material to improve life away from the computer. The elderly enjoy hunting for new recipes to try out, finding how-to videos to learn new hobbies and even finding exercises suitable for their limitations or tips for dealing with medical conditions.

Benefits of the computer

Being online obviously means having a computer and this also offers great potential for the elderly. Voice recognition software can deal with typing problems, pictures can be printed to show friends and they can download audio books to play back at their leisure. There is also a vast range of software offering games and entertainment, including puzzles specifically designed to keep the mind sharp.

And so the list goes on. The Internet has transformed life over the past decade. More than just helping your parents benefit from that, you will also be helping them feel less cut off from a society that can start to look as though it has left them behind.

How to get the elderly online

Okay, we're sold on the benefits but we have to be realistic. Whilst it's wrong to underestimate the potential of the elderly to embrace new technology, for many it's still a challenge, so how do we set about this?

Equipment

The starting point is ensuring they have the most appropriate computer. Laptops are convenient but the keyboards can be fiddly and screens are generally not that big. A good-sized screen is probably a sensible idea and if it has touch-screen technology that will make operating it even easier. It's also worth considering an ergonomic keyboard with wrist supports and an ergonomic mouse with wrist support pad.

As far as possible you should go for wireless technology, which eliminates tangles of wires. Take care, of course, to ensure any essential wiring doesn't run the risk of becoming a tripping hazard!

It's actually possible to buy a specially simplified computer designed for the elderly. This is called SimplicITy and it strips down the functions of the computer to core areas such as the Internet and email. This takes out a lot of the confusion presented by all the different icons and options presented on a typical computer screen.

Learning

Once you have the computer it is going to take time to get your elderly parent up to speed. This can of course be done by you or friends and family. It's a case of putting yourself in your parents' position and imagining you don't know the first thing about computers – even what a mouse does! Take things in small stages and if your parent is able to write easily then it might be a good idea for them to write down the basics of your explanations. This not only gives them a reference point in their own words, the physical act of writing also aids the learning process.

This can also be a great way for your own children to interact with gran and grandad. They can find it a lot of fun teaching their grandparents how to get into a world which they naturally understand, though make sure you guide them about doing this in a patient and appropriate way!

Alternatively there are now a large number of computer courses available in the community specially designed for older people. Age UK works with the Digital Inclusion network to provide training courses for the elderly across the country. You can visit their site to find one near you: Age UK Computer Training Courses for the Elderly. You can also see what's available from the Digital Champions Network, a group of people and organisations dedicated to getting more people online. There are many other providers besides these, you simply need to search in your area.

If your elderly parent is in a retirement complex or home you should speak with the management about opportunities there. Maybe funds could be used to provide communal computers and there should certainly be the opportunity to have someone visit the complex to provide an introduction to senior surfing.

Once they're up and running with how to operate things it's worth taking some time to explore the potential with them. Show them some sites they would enjoy and search together so they develop an awareness of the possibilities.

There are a great many sites designed with the elderly in mind and a little research, keeping your parents' interests in mind, can provide a helpful package for them to start with. Stick these sites in their favourites list and your parents will have fantastic resources to begin their journey. A popular place which brings together many links to useful sites for the elderly is Silversurfers. net – that can be another excellent starting point.

It can take time for something so new to become familiar to your elderly parents, but the Internet has transformed the lives of many older people, combating depression and isolation. It's a fantastic resource and most definitely worth the effort.

⇨ The above information is reprinted with kind permission from Nobilis. Please visit www. nobilis.co.uk for further information on this and other subjects.

There, I've just booked a Vespa trip through Italy!

Go for it Gran!

83-year-old YouTube star leads the way online

There's nothing to stop old people getting online and Peter Oakley, an 83-year-old YouTube star, has the audience to prove it.

By Matt Warman, Consumer Technology Editor

Peter Oakley is a pensioner from Leicester. At 83, he's part of a growing population of older people, living alone and often lonely. Except Mr Oakley isn't lonely, in part because more than eight million people have seen the videos he has posted on YouTube. Perhaps unexpectedly, that means he's also a poster boy for tomorrow's 'Silver Surfer's Day' that aims to get more older people online.

Using the jocular 'handle' of Geriatric1927, Mr Oakley signed up to YouTube in 2006. Widowed in 1998, he says his aim in buying a computer was simply to communicate with new people and to make new friends. 'I thought having a computer and the Internet would enable me to have a life,' he says. 'That didn't really work because I went into chat rooms which were full of kids. But somebody mentioned YouTube. In everyday life, the old don't have communications with the young outside the family, but the Internet can address that.'

The Race Online 2012 charity, founded by the Internet entrepreneur, and the Government's 'UK digital champion', Martha Lane Fox, has recently introduced a range of refurbished computers for sale at less than £100 to help get people online. It has also signed up 100,000 people to volunteer from diverse companies and organisations. The aim is to open up new social avenues, new economic possibilities for users and new options for government to save money by dealing with citizens online. Mr Oakley hails these as positive developments.

'The Internet is a wonderful tool for information, education and communication,' he says. 'I work with a friend in America who gives instructional lessons to his friends in a community centre, and has organised high-school students to come and give lessons one to one, and he reports the wonderful friendships that have developed between the old and the young.'

The project is the sort of thing Lane Fox hopes can help her initiative to achieve its aims. Research by the BBC indicates that people are more likely to try the Internet for the first time if a 'friendly face' helps show them what to do and what the benefits can be. John Lewis, Age UK and BT join the Scouts and Mecca Bingo among the 1,100 partners that Race Online 2012 has signed up to help with the campaign.

Substantial savings can be made by shopping online, too. As an example, new users of the web can typically save £200 per year by switching their home insurance. In this way, the Race Online machines can effectively pay for themselves.

Mr Oakley says that going online should no longer be frightening. 'Fear really, and embarrassment, is what's stopping people of my age,' he says. 'My peers feel they're left behind, that they can't possibly understand iPads and iPhones, and would feel too embarrassed about their inadequacies to take the plunge. I believe it's within families that we can make breakthroughs – encouraging older people's relatives to help.

'YouTube now has a nice platform that is a mixture of the old and the young.' Through his videos, talking to younger people about his long life, Oakley himself has brought about change. 'Proud isn't the right word, but I was responsible for that,' he says.

Perhaps unsurprisingly, YouTube has also paid Mr Oakley back. Although he says any advertising revenue is minuscule – 'My videos' views are going down,' he says, 'I've had my 15 minutes' – he has met both the Queen and Queen Rania of Jordan, when they visited Google events.

Mr Oakley is convinced that more reliance on the web is 'the way computers will go'. He believes that Google's new Chromebook computers will offer easier, more secure access to the web, for all generations. 'Chromebook will be a revolution in new ways of computing,' he says.

Do new products, however, offer real hope for the excluded final third that Lane Fox's campaign has focused on so intently? 'Race Online aims to solve the critical social and economic issues that arise when people are left behind as technology advances,' she says. By 2012, the aim is that, of the nine million people not online last year, the UK will be close to halving that number.

And for YouTube star Mr Oakley, there's a real human impact to the Internet, too. 'You have the access to many, many friends online,' he says. 'You watch and enjoy. I've made friends. And YouTube's where everybody goes to find anything out. There's even a video on how to breed earthworms. There's nothing that has been done that isn't online.'

When even octogenarians are telling their peers to log on and computers cost less than £100, excuses are few and far between.

19 May 2011

What can go wrong?

Information from CEOP.

Putting stuff up online that you wish you hadn't...

It's so easy to post online now - from your computer, digital camera or mobile, that often we do so without thinking. Sometimes we post things we wish we hadn't and want to get them removed. Most sites will have a delete post option, but remember that once you have put something up – anyone can save it and re-post.

Video hosting sites like YouTube do have the ability to take down inappropriate or offensive content. The video will need to be illegal or to have broken the terms and conditions of the site. On YouTube you can report by creating an account and logging in, once you have done this – you can 'flag content as inappropriate'. This option can be found under the video itself.

Some people without good intentions can try to persuade you to post inappropriate or sexual content online either via your digital camera, phone or on webcam. If you feel uncomfortable about anything that anyone asks you to do online, in a chat area, IM, social networking site or elsewhere – block them and then report it. You don't have to do anything you don't want to – even if you have done it before; so be strong with these people and say no if your instincts tell you it's not right.

Seeing things you wish you hadn't

The web is open for anyone to post material on it and that means sometimes there are things that you'll see, which you wish you hadn't.

If you see something that you just don't like, just close the screen on your laptop or turn off the monitor and go and tell an adult you trust. If there's no one around, close the site using the cross at the top of the browser. If you think the content might be illegal, like racist hate sites or pictures of children being abused you can report it directly to an organisation called the Internet Watch Foundation: www.iwf.org.uk. If the thing you don't like is a person – for example, someone exposing themselves on webcam or sending you indecent pictures – you can report that to CEOP and we will help.

Talking to weirdos

Unfortunately, as well as great people, there are some really strange people who use the Internet – people who aren't friendly or who have bad intentions. If someone is being inappropriate; saying sexual things or asking you to do things that you feel are wrong, start by saving the conversation, blocking them and then report it to CEOP using 'CEOP report'. Sometimes, people can seem really friendly and then do things which make you question the friendship and make you feel weird.

Feeling pressured to do things you don't want to

People who are looking to abuse young people online will often manipulate relationships and pressure you into doing things you feel uncomfortable with. Examples of this can include talking in a way that you don't like, asking you to do things on webcam or with your camera that feel wrong or uncomfortable or making you feel anxious or trapped in a romantic or sexual relationship.

The first thing to realise about this kind of relationship is that it is wrong. Adults who pressure young people into doing anything that they don't feel comfortable with should be reported using 'CEOP report' and blocked. They can be very clever and make you feel as though you have to do something because you owe them, or because otherwise they will get you in trouble.

This is wrong and you should report them.

Will I get in trouble?

NO!

You need to know that you won't be in trouble, whatever you have done. These adults are sometimes very skilful at making those they abuse or try to build a relationship with, feel guilty about what has happened. They do this to try and make the young person keep quiet about what has happened. It can make you feel unsafe and dirty. If someone does this to you, the responsibility for what happened is theirs, not yours and you can talk it through with a number of different people.

⇨ The above information is reprinted with kind permission from Child Exploitation and Online Protection Centre (CEOP). Please visit ceop.police.uk for further information.

© CEOP Child Exploitation and Online Protection Centre

Internet safety

Tips to keep safe online.

By Christina Hughes

The Internet is an amazing place. It often seems like a vast, limitless resource for entertainment, learning and communication. While this is all very exciting, the Internet also houses dangers that everyone needs to be aware of. It is important that you know how to enjoy the Internet, while staying safe online. You could be at risk from abuse such as bullying, fraud or something much more serious. Unlike seeing someone face to face, on the Internet people can easily represent themselves as anything they like by lying about their age, occupation and intentions.

Social networking

In recent years social networking sites have become incredibly popular. It seems like almost everyone is part of a social networking site such as Facebook, MySpace, Bebo or Twitter: people 'liking statuses' and 'tweeting' is now an everyday occurance.

While most users are genuine, it can be easy to hide your real identity so you must be careful. Online it is possible to come into contact with people you would normally want to avoid.

The risks

Privacy

The mask of anonymity online, combined with the feeling of freedom, can lead some people to behave in ways that they wouldn't dream of in public.

They might:

⇨ say things to you online that they would never say face to face;

⇨ give out personal information, about themselves or others, that they would usually keep private.

⇨ For example, a young person wants to let their friends know about their upcoming birthday party so posts all the party information, publicly, on a social networking site. This leads to lots of people knowing about the party, not just the young person's friends. These uninvited guests show up and cause trouble by getting angry and refusing to leave. In the end, the police have to get involved to diffuse the situation and turn people away.

Cyber bullying

Cyber bullying is just like bullying in real life, just online instead. Cyberbullying makes victims feel very frightened and alone, and because it takes place online, the bully can hide and try not get caught.

⇨ Nasty comments about a person can be posted online, as well as images and videos without their permission – this can all make the victim feel rather frightened and upset.

⇨ Victims can experience harassment from within their own user profile, as cyber bullies can hack into a victim's personal account.

⇨ People think that they can hide and cover up their identity online, so sometimes a person who wouldn't normally bully anyone might do so online.

⇨ Often, cyber bullies feel braver because they think they cannot be seen and that their actions cannot be traced – this is not true! Cyber bullying can sometimes be the most traceable form of bullying because there is evidence that it happened.

Cyber stalking

Just like other forms of stalking, harassment on the Internet can be very frightening. Victims of cyber stalking tend to be female, but males can be victims too. A person may be being harassed by an ex-boyfriend or girlfriend who is upset that the relationship ended, for example, or just a purely online friendship that has turned sour. Sometimes cyber stalking is completely random, with one online stranger directing this behaviour towards another.

Inappropriate content

Even with parental controls in place, it is still often possible for anyone to access inappropriate content online. You should beware of the websites that you visit, as although the Internet is full of many nice, friendly websites, there are also just as many sites featuring sex, violence, drug abuse and other disturbing images and messages. Think before you click a link!

Online grooming

The Internet has allowed the way we communicate to evolve and now we can socially interact with ease through Internet chat programs and social networking sites. Although these are a great way to keep in touch with family and friends, it is also a tool used my paedophiles. These Internet predators use these means of communication to contact young people and pretend to be a young person themselves.

The term online grooming is used to describe inappropriate behaviour towards a young person, commonly leading to sexual advances. Even if nothing dangerous does happen, just knowing that you have had contact with a person like that can be extremely upsetting.

Identity theft

The more private information that you post online, the

higher the risk of identity theft is. It can be very tempting to share personal information about yourself on social networking sites, but it's best to be a bit cautious and refrain from giving anything personal out. Personal information includes your:

⇨ email address

⇨ telephone number

⇨ home address

⇨ any banking details.

If you share these details, it can lead you to becoming a victim of fraud. This is very serious so it is important that you know the risks. If someone steals your identity, then they can:

⇨ steal a lot of money

⇨ commit crimes that could put you or your family in danger

⇨ commit crimes that could get you into trouble

Making 'friends'

We all know that spending hours and hours in front of a computer screen is not healthy. But there is a large amount of pressure from social networking sites to make sure you have lots of 'friends'. However, it is important to remember:

⇨ Real friendships are made through talking and sharing experiences, not by clicking a button.

⇨ By comparison, being online 'friends' is much less meaningful that a face-to-face relationship.

⇨ It is often all too easy to misunderstand a comment and fall out with an online 'friend'.

⇨ It is far easier, and healthier, to sort out problems face-to-face.

So, although you may know someone who boasts about having plenty of 'friends' on a social networking site, remember that these are not necessarily real friends.

Tips so you stay safe on social networking sites

⇨ Ensure that you are old enough to join.

⇨ Make up a nickname to use on your profile.

⇨ Never give out personal information.

⇨ Do not make friends with people you don't already know personally.

⇨ Perhaps use an email address that does not include your name.

⇨ Always use a 'strong' password. This means that you shouldn't use any names or words that someone might guess, like the name of your pet or your favourite band. Use a combination of random letters or numbers and regularly change your password.

⇨ Use the highest privacy setting when you set up your profile. This way only your friends can view your information.

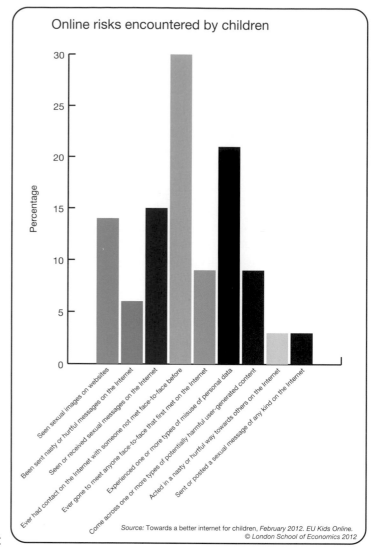

Online risks encountered by children

Source: Towards a better internet for children, February 2012. EU Kids Online.
© London School of Economics 2012

⇨ Be careful what you upload to the Internet. It is all too easy to share images and videos. Even if you only share a photo with a friend, it could be passed on and on.

⇨ Illegal downloads are best avoided. Be wary about sharing online content, especially if it isn't yours.

⇨ Never meet up with anyone that you have met online.

⇨ Be well informed about the safety features on a website. For example, some have a 'panic button' which can be clicked to escape the page quickly in case you see something you don't like.

⇨ If anything happens online that you don't like, tell someone.

13 August 2012

⇨ The above information is reprinted with kind permission from the author Christina Hughes.

© 2012 Christina Hughes

Go online in 2012 and have fun – but think safety first

With more than 1,000 reports a month from the public and industry, including around a quarter relating to online grooming, the Child Exploitation and Online Protection (CEOP) Centre is urging parents to help in keeping their children safe in 2012.

CEOP's reports can involve Internet abuse, making arrangements to meet a child online or a child in immediate danger.

The New Year will see more and more children go online, many for the first time using Christmas gifts of laptops, games consoles or mobile phones.

The Internet is essential for the UK's children, with latest OFCOM findings revealing that 95 per cent of 12–15-year-olds now have Internet access at home through a PC or laptop (up from 89 per cent in 2010). Over two in five 12–15s have a smartphone, with social networking one of the most popular activities, undertaken by 50% of teen smartphone owners on a regular basis. Yet many children and young people still go online, without thinking about the consequences of their actions.

Peter Davies, CEO of CEOP and ACPO lead for child protection commented:

'The Internet offers some fantastic opportunities for young people to learn, socialise with friends and explore their interests. All we are saying is have fun online and enjoy the benefits the Internet can bring, but in these early stages we ask parents to talk to their child and make sure their online safety is built in to everything they do. Every day we see the effects on children's lives when things do go wrong, so please work with us to keep our children safe and empower them to know what to do if things go wrong.'

Giving out too much personal information, posting inappropriate photos and comments and befriending people they don't know in the real world can put children at risk of bullying, or even contact, from people who may cause them harm. The effects can be and often are devastating.

In the same way children should be wary of unwanted approaches from strangers in the real world, they should also be careful if approached in the online world. The anonymity of the Internet can encourage children and young people to take risks or act in a way they would not normally – this can make them vulnerable to people who wish them harm so they need to think carefully about what they are doing online.

That's why CEOP are today encouraging parents not to be intimidated by the technology or the risks children may face, which can often be the case in stopping parents from talking to their children. They can find up-to-date advice and guidance on CEOP's website – www.thinkuknow.co.uk – a great place to get information on a range of issues, enabling parents to work through them with their children.

CEOP's ClickCEOP button can be used by a young person or an adult on their behalf, to report any concerns or suspicious online behaviour of another user. All reports are sent straight to specially trained officers at CEOP and dealt with on a case-by-case basis. this button can be found on many sites including MSN windows live messenger and within CEOP's 'ClickCEOP' profile in Facebook.

4 January 2012

⇨ The above information is reprinted with kind permission from Child Exploitation and Online Protection Centre (CEOP). Please visit ceop.police.uk for further information.

Internet safety: 'Sexting' a growing threat to children

Two schools a week are asking for help from an online safety group over concerns that pupils are 'sexting'.

By Amy Glendinning

The trend sees girls texting, emailing or uploading indecent images of themselves to boys or onto social networking sites. The images – often sexually graphic – are then passed around pupils, with or without the girls' permission. Sometimes the girls are persuaded to send pictures by a boyfriend – but others do it by choice to attract attention, unaware of the danger they place themselves in.

Staff at the e-safety group of Oldham Safeguarding Children's Board – who work across Greater Manchester – say on average two schools a week contact them for help with the problem and the number is on the increase. There is also concern that girls younger than ever are sexting – with the group recently dealing with its first case of a primary school pupil sending out explicit photos of themselves.

Other cases from schools in Greater Manchester over the last 12 months have included:

⇨ A girl who sent her boyfriend Sam an explicit picture of herself. Sam has now put the picture up as his Blackberry profile allowing anyone he messages to see it.

⇨ A learning mentor at a secondary school who discovered that two young girls had been videoed by older boys performing a sex act on them. The videos were being shared around school.

⇨ A girl who sent naked pictures of herself to her boyfriend at a sixth-form college. He shared them with a few of his closest friends to show off, then one of them posted the pictures online.

⇨ A 16-year-old who was seeing a boy for six months, but no-one in her family knew. Her sister found out the boy had posted pictures on Facebook of them together, with one showing her partially undressed. The girl was left terrified what her older brother might do if he sees the pictures.

⇨ A year nine boy who was pushed into the girls' changing room at the end of PE. Some of the other boys photographed it on their phones and put the pictures on Flickr. The pictures show girls who were changing.

⇨ A girl with learning difficulties who was sexually exploited by youths on her estate who created a Facebook page for her so that she can share pictures with them.

Teachers and social workers face an additional hurdle when girls come to them for help because it is technically illegal for them to search for the images.

David Barter, chair of the e-safety group, said: 'We are dealing with an awful lot of cases of sexting – it really is a growth area and something schools have to deal with so much more now. About two schools a week are contacting us at the moment for advice and we recently dealt with our first case of a primary school pupil sexting.

'Girls can be persuaded to send images to a boyfriend, but others do it out of choice, sending it to a boy they like or just uploading it to Facebook for anyone to see.

'There's a perception amongst teenagers that it's almost a form of "safe sex" – but they are putting themselves in danger of being targeted by paedophiles. Also, once the image is sent they can never get it back and they have no control over who sees it.

'It's very difficult for teachers or social workers to deal with because these pictures can be so explicit that if you searched for it or viewed it, you would be breaking the law.'

Part of the e-safety group's work is to advise and train adults on how to deal with sexting – emphasising that it is a personal problem, not purely a technology issue. They are also keen to emphasise to teenage boys that they have a responsibility not to share photos sent to them – as it can have devastating consequences.

Ten minutes to find photos of 15-year-old Cyrus on the Internet

Mum Emma Chadwick volunteered to let the MEN see how much we could find out about her son through his life online as part of our Internet safety series. In just TEN minutes, the *Manchester Evening News* was able to trace a surprising amount of information about Cyrus Bulsara.

We learned what school the 15-year-old student attended, along with photos of him on several Internet sites. Pictures were available on his Facebook page, his school's website, image-sharing website Flickr and a friend's blog.

Our findings left Emma, 45, shocked.

Emma, who lives with George in Manchester city centre and runs her own PR company, said: 'It is definitely worrying that you can find photos of him in just ten minutes.

'I didn't think you could do that if you weren't friends with him on Facebook so it is definitely something to think about.

'I think I would be more worried about it if he was younger.

'There's a lot of pressure for children to go on Facebook, and we have had conversations about what kind of information you should share on those sites.

'Now he's 15 I think he is old enough to be on Facebook – it's a cheap way for him to keep in touch with friends – but if he was younger I would be more worried about it.'

'Sexting' threat is lagging behind the law

A top legal expert says incidents of women and girls being blackmailed through explicit photos has previously gone 'under the radar' of the law.

Nazir Afzal, Chief Crown Prosecutor for the Crown Prosecution Service in the North West, says the issue of 'sexting' has previously passed legislators by. However, he says new guidance on cyber-stalking means the problem should now receive greater attention. It means prosecutors will now be given better guidance on the effects of stalking on victims and will be able to bring stronger cases against people who harass and try to blackmail people with threats of sharing photos.

Mr Afzal said: 'Police and prosecutors have begun to work even closer with victims' charities to identify the issues that have previously operated under the radar.

'This problem was one that perhaps passed us by, but victims can be assured that following the CPS' launch of guidance on tackling stalking and cyber-stalking we will work even harder to protect them from those who play on the vulnerability of some women and girls in the multi-media age.

'Too many young women are being tempted, cajoled through peer pressure or tricked into sending the most compromising photographs to virtual strangers or to partners in short-term relationships.

'I have seen the devastating impact that this can have where money or favours, including sexual ones, are demanded to prevent further disclosure.

'We are part of a generation encouraged to share pictures on Facebook and other social networks.

'We cannot stop the tide, but we can educate and advise. We can explain the dangers to privacy, the potential of you being a victim of blackmail and worse.'

14 April 2012

⇨ The above information is reprinted with kind permission from the *Manchester Evening News*. Please visit www.menmedia.co.uk for further information.

Self-taken images – 'sexting'

Information from CEOP.

Someone taking an indecent image of themselves, and sending it to their friends or boy/girlfriend via a mobile phone or some other form of technology is sometimes referred to as 'sexting'.

Once these images have been taken and sent to others, control is lost of them and they can end up anywhere. They could be seen by friends and family, a future employer, or even, in some cases, end up in the possession of an offender!

This also puts that person who originally sent the images in a vulnerable position, as somebody they may or may not know now has these images and could use technology to bully, harass or even try to locate them.

Just think – if you wouldn't print and pass these images around your school or show your mum or dad, they are not appropriate to share via phone or other technologies.

What can I do?

If you receive an indecent image or text from someone, do not send this image on to others. You will need to report it to a responsible adult.

If you know that an indecent image of you or a friend has been posted in the online environment, you will need to contact the service provider, such as Facebook, or YouTube to have it removed. You can do this by visiting their safety centres and following their reporting links.

The law

By sending indecent pictures of a person under 18 on to someone else you could be breaking the law.

If a teenager were to have in their possession an indecent image of another minor, they would technically be in possession of an indecent image of a child, which is an offence under the Protection of Children Act 1978 and the Criminal Justice Act 1988.

Who should I tell?

Always tell an adult you trust. This could be your mum, dad, school teacher or a cool auntie!

If somebody you don't know has contacted you inappropriately or the images are being used against you, fill out a report form at ClickCEOP.

If you are upset or worried by an image you have sent or received, you can call ChildLine and talk to someone in confidence on 0800 1111.

You can also visit www.cybermentors. org.uk for online support and advice about cyberbullying and much more.

⇨ The above information is reprinted with kind permission from Child Exploitation and Online Protection Centre (CEOP). Please visit ceop. police.uk for further information.

Preventing cyberbullying

Top ten tips for teens.

By Sameer Hinduja, Ph.D. and Justin W. Patchin, Ph.D.

Educate yourself

To prevent cyberbullying from occurring you must understand exactly what it is. Research what constitutes cyberbullying, as well as how and where it is most likely to occur. Talk to your friends about what they are seeing and experiencing.

Protect your password

Safeguard your password and other private information from prying eyes. Never leave passwords or other identifying information where others can see it. Also, never give out this information to anyone, even your best friend. If others know it,

take the time to change it now!

Keep photos PG

Before posting or sending that sexy image of yourself, consider if it's something you would want your parents, grandparents and the rest of the world to see. Bullies can use this picture as ammunition to make life miserable for you.

Never open unidentified or unsolicited messages

Never open messages (emails, text messages, Facebook messages, etc.) from people you don't know, or from known bullies. Delete them without reading. They could contain viruses that automatically infect your device if opened. Also never click on links to pages that are sent from someone you don't know. These too could contain a virus designed to collect your personal or private information.

Log out of online accounts

Don't save passwords in form fields within web sites or your web browser for convenience, and don't stay logged in when you walk away from the computer or cell phone. Don't give anyone even the slightest chance to pose as you online through your device. If you forget to log out of Facebook when using the computer at the

library, the next person who uses that computer could get into your account and cause significant problems for you.

Pause before you post

Do not post anything that may compromise your reputation. People will judge you based on how you appear to them online. They will also give or deny you opportunities (jobs, scholarships, internships) based on this.

Raise awareness

Start a movement, create a club, build a campaign, or host an event to bring awareness to cyberbullying. While you may understand what it is, it's not until others are aware of it too that we can truly prevent it from occurring.

Set-up privacy controls

Restrict access of your online profile to trusted friends only. Most social networking sites like Facebook and Google + offer you the ability to share certain information with friends only, but these settings must be configured in ordered to ensure maximum protection.

Google yourself

Regularly search your name in every major search engine (e.g., Google, Bing, Yahoo). If any personal information or photo comes up which may be used by cyberbullies to target you, take action to have it removed before it becomes a problem.

Don't be a cyberbully yourself

Treat others how you would want to be treated. By being a jerk to others online, you are reinforcing the idea that the behaviour is acceptable.

January 2012

⇨ The above information is reprinted with kind permission from the Cyberbullying Research Center. www.cyberbullying. us

What is cybercrime?

You hear a lot about cybercrime, but what exactly is it? The simple answer is, 'It's complicated!'

Like traditional crime, cybercrime can take many shapes and can occur nearly anytime or anyplace. Criminals committing cybercrime use a number of methods, depending on their skill-set and their goal. This should not be surprising: cybercrime is, after all, simply 'crime' with some sort of 'computer' or 'cyber' aspect.

⇨ Cybercrime has surpassed illegal drug trafficking as a criminal moneymaker.*

⇨ Every three seconds an identity is stolen.**

⇨ Without security, your unprotected PC can become infected within four minutes of connecting to the Internet.***

The Council of Europe's Cybercrime Treaty uses the term 'cybercrime' to refer to offenses ranging from criminal activity against data to content and copyright infringement [Krone, 2005]. However, others [Zeviar-Geese, 1997–98] suggest that the definition is broader, including activities such as fraud, unauthorised access, child pornography, and cyberstalking. The *United Nations Manual on the Prevention and Control of Computer- Related Crime* includes fraud, forgery, and unauthorised access [United Nations, 1995] in its cybercrime definition.

As you can see from these definitions, cybercrime can cover a very wide range of attacks. Understanding this wide variation in types of cybercrime is important as different types of cybercrime require different approaches to improving your computer safety.

Symantec draws from the many definitions of cybercrime and defines it concisely as any crime that is committed using a computer or network, or hardware device. The computer or device may be the agent of the crime, or may be the agent of the crime, the facilitator of the crime, or the target of the crime. The crime may take place on the computer alone or in addition to other locations. The broad range of cybercrime can be better understood by dividing it into two overall categories, defined for the purpose of this research as Type I and Type II cybercrime.

Type I cybercrime has the following characteristics:

⇨ It is generally a single event from the perspective of the victim. For example, the victim unknowingly downloads a Trojan horse which installs a keystroke logger on his or her machine. Alternatively, the victim might receive an email containing what claims to be a link to a known entity, but in reality is a link to a hostile website.

⇨ It is often facilitated by crimeware programs such as keystroke loggers, viruses, rootkits or Trojan horses.

⇨ Software flaws or vulnerabilities often provide the foothold for the attacker. For example, criminals controlling a website may take advantage of a vulnerability in a web browser to place a Trojan horse on the victim's computer.

Examples of this type of cybercrime include but are not limited to: phishing, theft or manipulation of data or services via hacking or viruses, identity theft, and bank or e-commerce fraud.

Type II cybercrime, at the other end of the spectrum, includes, but is not limited to activities such as cyberstalking and harassment, child predation, extortion, blackmail, stock market manipulation, complex corporate espionage, and planning or carrying out terrorist activities. The characteristics of Type II cybercrime are:

⇨ It is generally an on-going series of events, involving repeated interactions with the target. For example, the target is contacted in a chat room by someone who, over time, attempts to establish a relationship. Eventually, the criminal exploits the relationship to commit a crime. Or, members of a terrorist cell or criminal organisation may use hidden messages to communicate in a public forum to plan activities or discuss money laundering locations, for example.

⇨ It is generally facilitated by programs that do not fit into under the classification crimeware. For example, conversations may take place using IM (instant messaging) clients or files may be transferred using FTP.

References

*Cyber crime more profitable than drugs, NineMSN

**Identity Theft Statistics, Identity Protection Online

***Eliminating the Mobile Security Blind Spot, TechNewsWorld

Krone, T., 2005. *High Tech Crime Brief*. Australian Institute of Criminology. Canberra, Australia. ISSN 1832-3413. 2005.

Zeviar-Geese, G., 1997–98. The State of the Law on Cyberjurisdiction and Cybercrime on the Internet. California Pacific School of Law. *Gonzaga Journal of International Law.* Volume 1. 1997–1998.

⇨ The above information is reprinted with kind permission from the Symantec Corporation. Please visit www.uk.norton.com for further information.

© 1995 – 2012
Symantec Corporation

Frequently asked questions about the Internet

Information from The i in online.

When I publish information on the web, who does it belong to?

Read privacy statement and terms and conditions, this should inform you.

Who owns an image/photograph of me that is posted online?

The person who took the photo owns it unless they have agreed something different.

Who owns the rights over an image of me that I have placed online?

Unless you have signed website terms of use that say something different, then you own the rights over an image that you have placed online. Note that many websites have terms of use that say that anything that you post will belong to them so take care!

If I post an anonymous comment on somebodies page, can they find out who I am?

Yes they can, via the IP address. An IP address of the computer that you used to access the site will be available to the site owner. This could be used to trace you.

How do I delete information online?

Who published it? If you were not the person who posted the information then ask them to remove it, see below on how to find the website owner. If this is inappropriate, then you could speak to the service provider.

What can be done if I upload an image online without that person's consent?

You should always, always ask for the person's consent before posting information online. Once an image is uploaded, it is no longer private and could end up anywhere. So it is important to be aware of your privacy settings and the access other users may have to your page.

What should I do if a company requests information to send advertising material?

Make sure you trust the company; normally you have a choice. It is important to check the privacy policy of the company and look at how they intend to use your information? Does it explicitly state that the information will be kept confidential and not handed over to a third party?

How can I prevent receiving unsolicited emails?

You have the right to object to the processing of your data for the purposes of direct marketing. Speak to your Internet service provider and ask them to install a mail filter or contact one of the associations devoted to preventing junk email, e.g. www.spamfree.org

Your phone provider gave information about you to another company and you now receive unsolicited phone calls and/or emails. What can you do?

If information was collected for billing purposes alone and you did not consent to a further transfer of your data, you are entitled to object to the transfer of your data to any third party. First write to your provider stating your complaint and if the problem persists,

contact the national supervising authority.

How can I reduce my chances of identity theft?

Be careful about the information that you share online, for instance, address, date of birth, passwords, logon details, photos.

⇨ Ensure that you use a secure network.

⇨ Be wary of using public computers to access sensitive information such as logging onto online banking.

⇨ Choose good, strong passwords using a mixture of letters and numbers.

⇨ Do not use words that can be easily guessed or passwords that can be found in a dictionary.

What is phishing?

Phishing is an attempt to gain information using emails and websites that impersonate a genuine one, for instance an email from a bank, or other service provider.

⇨ Do not reply, this will show your email address to be valid.

⇨ Do not use any links contained within the email.

⇨ Do not be tricked into providing your logon details/password or other sensitive data, genuine banks will not ask you to tell them your login or password details.

⇨ Information from the i in online. Visit www.theiinonline.org.

© Speechly Bircham LLP 2010

Online reputation

Information from the UK Safer Internet Centre.

What is my online reputation?

Your online reputation is the perception, estimation and opinion that is formed when you are encountered online. This could be when someone visits your social networking profile, but could also be when anyone reads a comment you posted on another profile. It could also be when someone sees your online photo albums or an image with you in it, indeed any instance or reference of you that either you posted or someone else did – what your digital footprint says about you.

Your online reputation will be formed through:

⇨ Postings by you

⇨ Postings by others but about you or linked to you

⇨ Postings by others pretending to be you.

Who does it affect?

Everyone! Obviously it applies to those who post online; however, as other people could be posting information about you, you don't even have to have been on the Internet before to have an online reputation! Rory Cellan-Jones commented on a survey conducted by AVG which concluded that 23% of unborn children already have a digital footprint.

Why is online reputation important?

Many businesses and celebrities value their online identity and reputation and go to extraordinary lengths to protect it, in many cases taking legal action.

Your reputation should be important to you as it is a tool that others could and will use to make decisions about you. Clearly this could have a dramatic effect on your personal and professional lives, especially if your digital footprint is poor. Would you like a potential partner or employer to decide whether to see you or not purely based on your digital footprint? Media headlines regularly appear, such as the 'Disgrace of the six drinking, pole-dancing primary school teachers who published the pictures on Facebook' (Source: *Daily Mail*).

What does your profile picture or avatar say about you?

How is your online reputation different?

Remember that the Internet never forgets – when you post something online it will always be there.

What the research says

Microsoft published two studies to coincide with Data Privacy Day in 2010 (conducted by Cross Tab Marketing Services) looking at the influence of online information as part of job applications and also consumer attitudes to online reputation.

'23% of unborn children already have a digital footprint'

Extracts from the studies concluded that:

⇨ 83% of consumers polled said they believe they have some control over their online reputation, but less than half consider their reputation every time they post information. Only 32% consider the reputations of others.

⇨ 47% of UK employers use publicly available online information when examining potential job candidates (79% in the US and 59% in Germany).

⇨ 41% of employers have rejected candidates based on their online reputation (70% in the US). Only 9% of candidates in the UK think prospective employers do this.

⇨ Mostly employers use search engines (78%) or social networking sites (63%).

⇨ The most common reason (57%) that a candidate was rejected in the UK was through 'inappropriate comments or text written by the candidate'. In the US the highest (58%) was concerns about the candidate's lifestyle.

'41% of employers have rejected candidates based on their online reputation'

Other examples of reasons for rejection in the UK:

⇨ 51% unsuitable photos or video

⇨ 40% comments criticising previous employers, co-workers or clients

⇨ 37% inappropriate comments posted by colleagues or work acquaintances

⇨ 35% inappropriate comments posted by friends or relatives

⇨ 33% membership of certain groups

⇨ 18% concern about the candidates financial background.

What can I do? Strategies for managing your online reputation

⇨ Think before you post anything

⇨ Understanding your digital footprint

  ⇨ Search for yourself using Google or another search provider

⇨ Appropriate language and behaviour

  ⇨ Consider how others may interpret your words, especially if using abbreviations

⇨ Protect your passwords

  ⇨ Don't disclose and the stronger the better! www.pctools.com/guides/password/

⇨ Managing your Privacy settings, using privacy effectively

⇨ Testing your privacy

  ⇨ Find out from your friends what information they can see on your profile? Use http://www.reclaimprivacy.org/ to scan your profile privacy settings

⇨ Discussing expectations with friends

  ⇨ Are you happy to be tagged in a photo?

⇨ Familiarise yourself with your organisation's policies and procedures

  ⇨ Make sure you know how what the rules are!

More sophisticated ways to consider amending your Digital footprint:

⇨ Limiting your online information in Google searches

⇨ Removing yourself from Facebook searches

⇨ Manage your friends lists and redefining access you allow to your content

⇨ Manage your online photos and albums

⇨ Explore what other applications access your online profiles

⇨ Does your physical location appear online?

⇨ Look for photos you are 'tagged' in

⇨ Regularly review your privacy settings and amend accordingly.

'Regularly review your privacy settings and amend accordingly'

When posting online consider:

⇨ Scale – global platforms

⇨ Permanency – once it is online it is there forever

⇨ Audience – public or private? friends, friends of friends or everyone?

Use the technology to its full potential but just be aware of the pitfalls and think before you post.

⇨ The above information is reprinted with kind permission from the UK Safer Internet Centre. Please visit www.saferInternet.org.uk for more information.

© UK Safer Internet Centre

Children and online privacy survey

Information from The i in online.

The i in online data provides a large population (4,116 in total) analysis on the behaviours and attitudes of young people towards online technology and privacy. Some headline statistics confirm our beliefs around such matters:

⇨ children and young people readily engage with online social media

⇨ sometimes they struggle with the policies that are supposed to be in place to protect them

⇨ they are aware of the need to protect their data, but are not always equipped to do so.

'32% said they didn't know what a privacy policy was'

Our respondents were asked whether they engaged in any social networking activities themselves. In total 69% of our respondents said they did use social networking sites. There were some gender differences, with girls (72%) more likely to have a social networking profile than boys (65%).

The social network that is most popular is, unsurprisingly, Facebook, with 47% of respondents saying they had a Facebook profile. Again unsurprisingly, the vast majority of secondary school respondents (88%) had Facebook profiles. However, we also had over a third (39%) of young people of primary school age said they had Facebook profiles. Girls are slightly more likely (50% in total) to have Facebook profiles than boys (43%).

The second most popular social networking activity was MSN, with 20% of respondents using it. Girls are more likely (26%) than boys (15%) to use MSN. Somewhat surprisingly it was almost as likely for a young person of primary school age (21%) to use MSN as someone of secondary school age (27%).

Boys are also more likely (56%) than girls (33%) to have an avatar, a virtual representation of themselves. However, there is little evidence to show that having an avatar results in different behaviours or attitudes toward data protection.

Our respondents were asked whether they had ever read a privacy policy. In total 40% of respondents had, meaning 60% of young people have not read the privacy policies of the web sites they use. This statistic differed little between young people of primary and secondary school age, but girls were more likely (44%) than boys (35%) to read a privacy policy. Boys are likely to have a more relaxed attitude towards data and data sharing, although this is far from irresponsible with the vast majority still believing their data should only be seen by friends and family and parental consent was necessary in all scenarios presented about where their data might be exposed.

When those who had not read a policy were asked why not, there were a variety of responses. 32% said they didn't know what a privacy policy was, with 23% saying they didn't know where to find it. A quarter felt they were too complicated, and another quarter did not feel it important. Interestingly, more secondary school respondents (44%) felt they were too complicated, although more primary children didn't know what a privacy policy was (37%).

Those who had looked at privacy policies had divided opinions, with around half (51%) thinking they were easy to find and 57% understanding what was there. The vast majority (84%) looked at the policy because

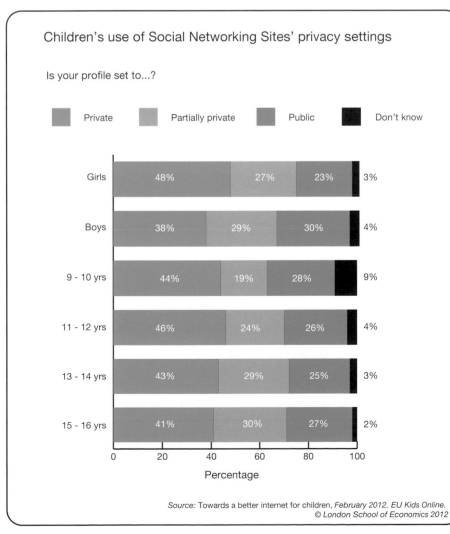

Children's use of Social Networking Sites' privacy settings

Is your profile set to...?

Private | Partially private | Public | Don't know

	Private	Partially private	Public	Don't know
Girls	48%	27%	23%	3%
Boys	38%	29%	30%	4%
9 - 10 yrs	44%	19%	28%	9%
11 - 12 yrs	46%	24%	26%	4%
13 - 14 yrs	43%	29%	25%	3%
15 - 16 yrs	41%	30%	27%	2%

Percentage

Source: Towards a better internet for children, *February 2012. EU Kids Online.*
© London School of Economics 2012

they thought it was an important thing to do. There was little statistical variation across the demographic groups for those who had looked at privacy policies.

'The social network that is most popular is, unsurprisingly Facebook'

So we had an interesting split in our population – those who do engage in privacy policies may understand what is presented and think they are important. However, the majority of our respondents hadn't seen a policy for a number of reasons. They were also asked what might be done to improve privacy policies and a large number of children said privacy policies should be made more simple with 'less words'.

However, it was also clear that our respondents felt that privacy on social networking was important, with the vast majority (85%) saying that social networks should have the strongest privacy settings by default and an even larger majority (94%) feeling that clear rules were needed to help with the removal of photos and videos posted without consent.

'While the use of social networking used to be considered something for secondary aged pupils our data shows that the majority of primary aged pupils also engage'

We can also show that under-aged Facebook users are responsible with their data and show little variation in attitude with those who do not use it. In addition, they are more likely to read privacy policies (48.8% of primary Facebook users compared to 39.6% of the total primary population) and be aware of why they are important.

What our data does clearly highlight is the need for education at a primary school level. While the use of social networking used to be considered something for secondary aged pupils our data shows that the majority of primary aged pupils also engage. However, it also shows that primary aged pupils are potential more vulnerable as a result of not being aware of privacy policy or where to find it. While they are generally more protective of their data, the change in attitude at secondary age does suggest that without effective education at a primary school level, there is potential for more risky behaviours in adolescent life.

The data also shows that while not all of our population felt privacy policies were complicated there was a great deal of confusion around them. They were also very clear that service providers should provide the most private settings by default. Clearly this is a population that feels service providers also have a responsibility to protect their data, but also provide policy and advice in a clear, understandable, and easy to find manner.

In conclusion, children and young people are very much engaged with digital technology and its social uses. However, there are still significant issues around education and practice to be addressed. While our population did not come across as naive around data protection issues, they were clearly not as well informed as they could be, and felt they needed help from service providers in ensuring 'their' data was protected.

The analysis of the data was conducted by Prof. Andy Phippen, Plymouth Business School, University of Plymouth.

July 2011

⇨ The above information is reprinted with kind permission from The i in online. Please visit www. theiinonline.org for further information.

What do children do online?

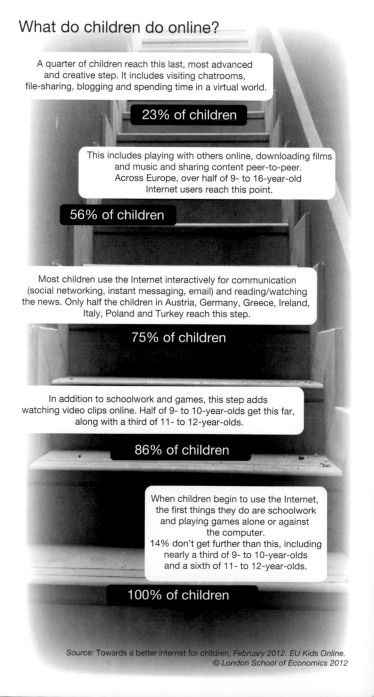

A quarter of children reach this last, most advanced and creative step. It includes visiting chatrooms, file-sharing, blogging and spending time in a virtual world.

23% of children

This includes playing with others online, downloading films and music and sharing content peer-to-peer. Across Europe, over half of 9- to 16-year-old Internet users reach this point.

56% of children

Most children use the Internet interactively for communication (social networking, instant messaging, email) and reading/watching the news. Only half the children in Austria, Germany, Greece, Ireland, Italy, Poland and Turkey reach this step.

75% of children

In addition to schoolwork and games, this step adds watching video clips online. Half of 9- to 10-year-olds get this far, along with a third of 11- to 12-year-olds.

86% of children

When children begin to use the Internet, the first things they do are schoolwork and playing games alone or against the computer. 14% don't get further than this, including nearly a third of 9- to 10-year-olds and a sixth of 11- to 12-year-olds.

100% of children

Source: Towards a better internet for children, February 2012. EU Kids Online.

SOPA and PIPA

The facts and the debate.

By Ian Stokes

Two acts put forward in the U.S. recently received a lot of media attention due to wide-scale protesting from some of the biggest names on the Internet. These acts, known as the Stop Online Piracy Act (SOPA) and the Protect IP Act (PIPA), caused a fierce debate over where the line between protecting copyright and protecting civil liberties lies. But why are SOPA and PIPA needed in the first place? What do they mean and why was there such a severe reaction to them when they were proposed?

The why

Copyright theft is estimated to cost the U.S. economy around $58 billion a year, and the U.S. Government is in a constant battle with pirates, at both a national and international level. However, whilst there are laws which allow them to seek out and punish both those providing illegal content and those accessing it within the U.S., they are less well equipped to combat websites based outside their borders.

If the U.S. Department of Justice suspects that a foreign website is breaking copyright law, they can call upon the government of the country where the website is based in to take action and shut them down. This was the case in the recent shutdown of Megaupload when the U.S. Government worked with both the authorities of Hong Kong and New Zealand to shut down Megaupload's servers and detain the founder, Kim Dotcom.

However, there are many countries who would not work with the U.S. in such matters, including China and North Korea. This hole in the U.S.'s crime fighting net led to the creation of SOPA and PIPA, bills aimed at foreign websites which commit copyright infringement.

The what

SOPA was put before the U.S. House of Representatives on 26 October 2011 by Lamar Smith, whilst its equivalent in the senate, PIPA, was put forward on 12 May 2011 by Patrick Leahy. Both bills are very similar in the powers they would bestow upon both the Department of Justice and those who hold the copyright themselves. However, SOPA has wider reaching implications as it applies to any 'U.S.-directed foreign Internet site committing or facilitating online piracy', whereas PIPA only applies to websites which have 'no significant use other than engaging in or facilitating copyright infringement'.

Both SOPA and PIPA allow the U.S. Department of Justice, or the intellectual property holder who is being harmed, to seek court orders which require advertising companies and payment providers to cease all business with the infringing site. It also requires search engines to remove the infringing site from its databases. So whilst the site could continue to operate, it would have no funding and would not be findable via search engine, essentially shutting down the site.

Search engines, payment providers and advertisers are immune to any liability providing they 'take actions required by this Act or otherwise voluntarily block access to or end financial affiliation with such sites'.

The opposition

SOPA and PIPA have received strong opposition from a number of companies and organisations. An open letter to Washington was signed by the founders of Google, Twitter, Yahoo!, YouTube, PayPal, eBay and Wikipedia amongst others, which stated their opposition to the two bills which would undermine the very framework of the Internet. Computing giant Microsoft kept quiet on the issue for some time but finally said, 'We oppose the passage of the SOPA bill as currently drafted.'

Celebrities too voiced their opinions, with messages on Twitter from Mark Zuckerberg (founder of Facebook), Kim Kardashian, Ashton Kutcher and even MC Hammer stating their opposition to SOPA. Adam Savage, of Mythbusters fame, went further and wrote an article for the website Popular Mechanics accusing SOPA of being 'a clear violation of our First Amendment right to free speech'.

Even the White House has voiced its opposition to the bills as they currently stand, saying in a statement that: 'While we believe that online piracy by foreign websites is a serious problem that requires a serious legislative response, we will not support legislation that reduces freedom of expression, increases cybersecurity risk or undermines the dynamic, innovative global Internet.'

...and their arguments

One of the biggest concerns people have about SOPA and PIPA is that they say the burden of proof lies with the accused, not the accuser. When a claim is made, the website can be cut off from payment providers, ad services and search engines without any prior notice to the accused website, giving them no time to dispute the claim or rectify the situation. Regardless of whether the claim was genuine or not, only the accused suffers any consequences.

There are also concerns about where this bill will lead to, with many fearing that SOPA and PIPA will open the gates for wider scale censorship of the Internet, a concept usually reserved for countries like Iran, North Korea and China.

The supporters

Support for SOPA and PIPA comes mainly from the entertainment industry, with the Motion Picture Association of America (MPAA), Recording Industry Association of America (RIAA) and Entertainment Software Association (ESA) all supporting the bill and the increased powers it gives to copyright holders. Whilst these names might not be recognisable at first, each of these organisations is made up of numerous member companies including Walt Disney, Paramount, Sony, Warner Bros, Nintendo, Sega and many more. Therefore, these three organisations represent almost the entire film, music and video games industry.

...and their arguments

Those supporting SOPA and PIPA say that it is necessary to protect the American economy, citing the billions of dollars lost in sales, tax and employee earnings every year. They also believe that the bills will put pressure on search engines and service providers, forcing them to better police the content that they allow users to view.

So where are SOPA And PIPA today?

The lines were drawn with Silicon Valley facing off against Hollywood, the tech industry against the entertainment industry, but what happened to SOPA and PIPA? On Wednesday 18 January, opponents of SOPA and PIPA staged a massive blackout, an event that is now called 'the day the Internet went dark'. Users who visited Wikipedia were greeted by a banner explaining the protest along with links to information about SOPA and PIPA. Google censored their logo with a black bar and started an online petition against SOPA and PIPA which gathered over seven million signatures. At least 115,000 other websites either blacked out or altered their home pages in the protest.

This dramatic event brought the issue into the spotlight as Senators and Representative's phone lines rang off the hook and websites were brought to a standstill by people trying to voice their opposition to the bills. Over the next two days several co-sponsors of SOPA and PIPA began to retract their support and many officials who had been undecided flocked to the opposition camp.

On Friday 20 January, Senate Majority Leader Harry Reid released a statement saying, 'In light of recent events, I have decided to postpone Tuesday's vote on the PROTECT IP Act.'

That same Friday morning, Lamar Smith announced that he was postponing the vote on SOPA, saying, 'It is clear that we need to revisit the approach on how best to address the problem of foreign thieves that steal and sell American inventions and products.'

It is important to note that neither of these bills are 'dead', they are simply no longer being considered in their current state. Lawmakers are working together with representatives from both the entertainment and tech industries in order to reach a compromise which can protect intellectual property without hampering civil rights.

August 2012

⇨ The above article is printed with kind permission from the author Ian Stokes.

© 2012 Ian Stokes

HM Government

e-petition

Responsible department: Department for Culture, Media and Sport

We stand for a Free and Open Internet (Declaration of Internet Freedom).

We believe that a free and open Internet can bring about a better world. To keep the Internet free and open, we call on the Government to recognise these principles. We believe that they will help to bring about more creativity, more innovation and more open societies.

We support transparent and participatory processes for making Internet policy and the establishment of five basic principles:

Expression: Don't censor the Internet.

Access: Promote universal access to fast and affordable networks.

Openness: Keep the Internet an open network where everyone is free to connect, communicate, write, read, watch, speak, listen, learn, create and innovate.

Innovation: Protect the freedom to innovate and create without permission. Don't block new technologies, and don't punish innovators for their users' actions.

Privacy: Protect privacy and defend everyone's ability to control how their data and devices are used.

Petition closes 5 July 2013

⇨ The above information is reprinted with kind permission from HM Government. Please visit epetitions.direct.gov.uk to sign this petition.

© Crown copyright

Is Internet access a human right?

As family life migrates online and the web becomes the home of free expression, it's getting harder for courts to prevent individuals going online.

A recent United Nations Human Rights Council report examined the important question of whether Internet access is a human right.

While the Special Rapporteur's conclusions are nuanced in respect of blocking sites or providing limited access, he is clear that restricting access completely will always be a breach of Article 19 of the International Covenant on Civil and Political Rights, the right to freedom of expression.

But not everyone agrees with the UN's conclusion. Vint Cerf, a so-called 'father of the Internet' and a vice-president at Google, argued in a *New York Times* editorial that Internet access is not a human right:

The best way to characterise human rights is to identify the outcomes that we are trying to ensure. These include critical freedoms like freedom of speech and freedom of access to information – and those are not necessarily bound to any particular technology at any particular time.

Indeed, even the United Nations report, which was widely hailed as declaring Internet access a human right, acknowledged that the Internet was valuable as a means to an end, not as an end in itself.

Cerf does concede that Internet access may be a civil right, defined as a right which is 'conferred upon us by law' (arguably a definition which does not apply to the UK where the European Convention on Human Rights has been incorporated into our law). He says:

While the US has never decreed that everyone has a 'right' to a telephone, we have come close to this with the notion of 'universal service' – the idea that telephone service (and electricity, and now broadband Internet) must be available even in the most remote regions of the country. When we accept this idea, we are edging into the idea of Internet access as a civil right, because ensuring access is a policy made by the government.

There have been some interesting responses to Cerf's op-ed. Amnesty

International's USA blog argues that he provides an 'exceptionally narrow portrayal of human rights from a legal and philosophical perspective'. Moreover, his means versus ends characterisation of rights is philosophically incoherent, for:

while access to the physical town square may not be a human right in isolation, it has always been for most inseparable from the right to association and expression

So, applying the same logic, Internet access is inseparable from freedom of expression and its lesser spotted cousin, freedom of access to information. Moreover, I would argue that Internet use may also fall within Article 8 ECHR, the right to family and private life, as email, Skype, Facebook and Twitter are now essential tools of interaction between friends and family.

From the technological stand-point, JD Rucker on the Techi Blog argues that outcomes are key, and elevating the Internet to the status of an inalienable right will result in 'increased opportunity, improved education, and the end of hostilities based upon ignorance'.

Matthew Ingram on GigaOM also makes the practical point that not defining Internet access as a human or civil right 'makes it easier for governments to place restrictions on access or even shut it down entirely'. This is particularly relevant given the widely-cited role of the Internet and specifically social media in recent political revolutions like the Arab Spring.

Of course, this is not just a philosophical debate. States already ban Internet use in one form or another regularly. Closer to home, there are already a number of laws which allow state authorities to restrict Internet access, most notably rules relating to sex offenders and terrorist suspects. The troubled Digital Economy Act has been attacked over proposed powers to ban websites which host copyright material without permission. The Government subsequently backed down over the issue, but the Act remains controversial.

Interestingly, the UK Court of Appeal has agreed with the sentiment of the UN report, although without expressing its conclusion in terms of human rights. The recent case of Regina v Smith & others involved an examination of the terms of a Sexual Offences Prevention Order under the Sexual Offences Act 2003.

The court ruled that the Internet was an 'essential part of everyday living' and therefore, a complete ban on use in this case would be disproportionate. This was expressed in very wide terms, and it is difficult to imagine many scenarios where a complete ban would be permitted by law. Lord Justice Hughes said:

Before the creation of the Internet, if a defendant kept books of pictures of child pornography it would not have occurred to anyone to ban him from possession of all printed material. The Internet is a modern equivalent.

However, full Internet bans have occasionally been permitted by the courts. Mr Justice Silber ruled

in the November 2011 case of AM v Secretary of State for the Home Department that a full Internet ban placed upon a terrorist suspect subject to a control order (a highly restrictive anti-terrorism power) was lawful. It should be noted that the successor to control orders, the TPIM, no longer permits complete Internet bans.

Interestingly, in AM the judge accepted the security services' evidence that it would be practically impossible to monitor the suspect's Internet use, due in part to vulnerabilities in the Windows operating system. This sounds highly debatable, but perhaps that technical argument will be had on another day.

Ultimately, it seems that the current position in UK law – reflecting but not wholly endorsing the UN report – is that Internet access will remain, reflecting freedom of expression under Article 10 ECHR, a qualified right. That is, it can be restricted but only if that restriction is provided for by law and necessary/proportionate in a democratic society, unlike for example the absolute restriction on inhuman and degrading treatment under Article 3 ECHR.

Indeed, the UN report accepts that in some scenarios Internet access will need to be restricted, for

example in the case of sex offenders and terrorist suspects.

This is a question which will certainly be revisited in the coming years. Whether the UN or Vint Cerf is right on a philosophical level as to whether Internet access should be characterised as a human right, technology is changing rapidly and the courts will have to do their best to keep up. Whether or not it is a human right in its own respect, the Internet provides the gateway to other freedoms, notably freedom of expression and the right to family and private life and therefore access to it can be, practically, inseparable from the rights themselves.

It is highly unlikely that Internet access will ever attain the status of an absolute right. However, the current position of UK courts rightly makes it very difficult indeed for the state to ban completely a citizen's use of the Internet, however strong the justification.

11 January 2012

⇨ The above article originally appeared in the *Guardian*. Please visit www.guardian.co.uk for further information.

Key Facts

- By August 2011, 77% of households [in the UK] were connected (up 4 percentage points on 2010), with 30 million going online every day or almost every day. (page 1)

- In 2009 23% went online with a phone. By 2010 it was 31%. In 2011 it was 45% ... By 2012 46% of Brits were using a smartphone. (page 1)

- We spend around 57 hours per month on computers. Roughly half that time is spent offline in Word and PowerPoint, organising photos, watching films and playing games. The rest is spent online. (pages 1 – 2).

- Globally, there are fewer women on the internet than men, but they spend more time on it. In the UK, women have overtaken men online (51.3% vs 48.7%) and reflect the broader pattern of heavier usage, spending about 8% more time online. (page 2)

- About 7% of adults fritter away their cash online and women are, in fact, more likely to visit some gambling sites than men (e.g. lotto and sweepstakes). (page 3)

- Over 90% of children have internet access at home and the majority also use the internet at school. The average 7 to 10-year-old now spends around 8 hours a week online, climbing to 18 hours a week for 11-14s and 24 hours a week for those aged 15-19. (page 4)

- The majority of consumers (81%) think it is everyone's right to have broadband at home, regardless of where they live. (page 6)

- Just over one in five UK adults (22%) in the UK still do not use the Internet at home. (page 6)

- Many young people are not careful when they use the Internet. They are often unable to find the information they are looking for or they trust the first thing they do find. (page 10)

- UK ICT education system is falling behind other countries such as South Korea, Israel and even Scotland – who are considered to be pioneers of teaching ICT. (page 13)

- An estimated five to ten per cent of internet users are thought to be addicted – meaning they are unable to control their use. The majority are games players who become so absorbed in the activity they go without food or drink for long periods and their education, work and relationships suffer. (page 18)

- Over 65s are the fastest growing age-group on Facebook and over 50s are joining Match.com faster than any other age group. (page 19)

- 95% of 12– to 15-year-olds now have Internet access at home through a PC. (page 25)

- Cybercrime has surpassed illegal drug trafficking as a criminal moneymaker – every 3 seconds an identity is stolen. (page 29)

- 23% of unborn children already have a digital footprint. (page 32)

- 41% of employers have rejected candidates based on their online reputation (70% in the US). Only 9% of candidates in the UK think prospective employers do this. (page 32)

- 83% of consumers polled said they believe they have some control over their online reputation, but less than half consider their reputation every time they post information. Only 32% consider the reputations of others. (page 32)

- According to The i in online, the most popular social networking site is Facebook (47% of survey respondents saying that they had a Facebook profile). Girls were slightly more likely to have a Facebook profile than boys (50% vs 43%). (page 33)

- The majority of people (85%) think that social networking sites should have the strongest privacy settings by default. (page 34)

Glossary

Avatar / Online persona

An image or character that is your visual representation to the online world.

Broadband Internet Access

Usually shorted to just broadband, this refers to the telecommunications signal which is of greater bandwidth than the standard/usual signal. The broader the band, the greater the capacity for traffic which means faster download speeds.

Cyberbullying

Cyberbullying is when technology is used to harass, embarrass or threaten to hurt someone. A lot is done through social networking sites such as Facebook, Twitter, MySpace and Bebo. Bullying via mobile phones is also a form of cyberbullying. With the use of technology on the rise, there are more and more incidents of cyberbullying.

Cybercrime

Crime with some kind of 'computer' or 'cyber' aspect to it: using modern telecommunication networks such as the Internet (like chat rooms, e-mails and forums) and mobile phones (texting) to intentionally psychically or mentally harm and cause distress. Computer viruses, cyberstalking, identity theft and phiching scams are some examples of cybercrime.

Digital footprint

The 'trail' a person leaves behind when they interact with the digital environment. This evidence left behind gives clues as to the person's existence, presence and identify. It also refers to what other people may say about you online, not just yourself: sometimes also referred to as your online presence.

Digital native

A person who has grown up surrounded by digital technology, such as mobile phones, computers and the Internet (the current 12- to 18-year-old generation).

E-tail

A play on the word 'retail', this refers to shopping online.

Internet

A worldwide system of interlinked computers, all communicating with each other via phone lines, satellite links, wireless networks and cable systems.

Social networking sites

A place online where people, usually with similar interests, hobbies or backgrounds, can build social networks and social relations together. Examples include websites such as Facebook, Twitter, Bebo and MySpace.

Sexting

Someone uploading and sending an indecent, usually sexually graphic, image to their friend or boy/girlfriend via mobile phone or the Internet.

Troll / Troller

Troll is Internet slang for someone who intentional posts something online to provoke a reaction. The idea behind the trolling phenomenon is that it is about humour, mischief, and some argue, freedom of speech; it can be anything from a cheeky remark to a violent threat. However, sometimes these internet pranks can be taken too far, such as a person who defaces Internet tributes site, causing the victims family further grief.

Phishing

A play on the word 'fishing'. This is where "bait", such an e-mail or instant message, is sent from someone pretending to be from a popular social network site, auction site, online payment processor (like PayPal) or an IT administrator. When the unsuspecting victim "bites", either by clicking a malicious link or opening a malicious attachment, their financial, password and personal information may then be stolen.

Stop Online Piracy Act (SOPA) and Protect IP Act (PIPA)

SOPA and PIPA are two acts that were put forward in the USA to help protect online copyright and against online copyright infringements. Both SOPA and PIPA would allow the U.S. Department of Justice, or the intellectual property holder who is being harmed, to seek court orders which require advertising companies and payment providers to cease all business with the infringing site, and for search engines to remove the offending site from their database.

Assignments

The following tasks aim to help you think through the debate surrounding the evolution of the Internet and provide a better understanding of the topic:

1. Look at some of the statistics from the article 'Digital Britain' on pages 1 to 5. Using these as a starting point to create your own questionnaire or survey about Internet usage in your class and create a graph from the results. You can ask people what kind of activities they do online and how much time they spend on the computer.

2. What is 'broadband'? Do you think it is essential for everyone? Discuss in small groups and feedback to the rest of your class.

3. 'Is Internet access a human right?' Stage a class debate, with half arguing for the motion and the other half against.

4. Create a Digital Literary Campaign for your school, including leaflets and a short speech. How important is it for children to be digital literate? Do you think it should be taught as part of the school curriculum?

5. Design a website to educate Internet users about cyberbullying, especially in relation to social networking sites and how to keep themselves safe online. Create a homepage, logo and three different detailed sections.

6. What types of technology might be used to bully someone? Create a list and then address each item in turn and find ways of how to protect yourself and keep safe whilst using that technological device.

7. Create a storyboard for a 30 second Youtube video explaining what 'sexting' is and how to handle situations involving 'sexting'. You should provide information on the effect that 'sexting' has on the victim and others impacted by it. Also include some details on how to stay safe when using a mobile phone. If you want to take this further, you could write a script and act out the video in small groups.

8. Read the article 'SOPA and PIPA' on page 35. What are SOPA and PIPA? What do they mean and why was there such a severe reaction to them when they were proposed?

9. Design a poster highlighting the dangers of Internet addiction. Be sure to include information about clear symptoms and the effects of Internet addition. You may wish to use the article 'Addicted! Scientists show how Internet dependency alters the human brain' on page 14 as a guide.

10. What would the world be like without the Internet? In groups, discuss this statement and then produce a presentation about your discussion results. How would communication differ? What kind of impact would it have on bullying? What about shopping?

11. Create a scheme which promotes teaching older people how to make use of the Internet. What kind of things would you teach the elderly? How would they benefit from using the Internet? How would you explain the concept of Facebook and setting up a profile to an older person?

12. Watch the 2010 film *Catfish* and write a blog entry discussing what it teaches us about online safety and social networking.

13. How do you think parents can protect their children online? Discuss this with a partner.

14. Read the petition for Internet freedom on page 37. Do you agree with the principal that the Internet should not be censored? Write a letter to your local MP arguing for or against the principles set out in the e-petition.

15. Imagine you live in a rural village in England that does not yet have broadband access. Write a letter to a friend explaining the effect this has on you, and what would be different if you were able to use broadband.

16. Imagine that the Internet does not exist. Using only books, newspapers or the library, research a historical figure of your choice. Write a report, roughly two sides of A4, on your chosen figure. When you have finished, write some notes on your experience. Was it more difficult to find information?

Acknowledgements

The publisher is grateful for permission to reproduce the following material.

While every care has been taken to trace and acknowledge copyright, the publisher tenders its apology for any accidental infringement or where copyright has proved untraceable. The publisher would be pleased to come to a suitable arrangement in any such case with the rightful owner.

Chapter One: Exploring the Internet

Digital Britain, © 2012 DARE, *Digital divide risks becoming a gulf*, © 2012 Communications Consumer Panel, *The broadband debate*, © International Telecommunication Union, *The Net Generation, unplugged*, © The Economist Newspaper Limited 2012, *Truth, lies and the Internet*, © 2011 Demos, *The changing face of digital literacy in UK schools and universities*, © 2012 Metia, *Addicted! Scientists show how Internet dependency alters the human brain*, © The Independent, *New research about Facebook addiction*, © University of Bergen, *Internet addiction: the next new fad diagnosis*, © 2012 AOL (UK) Limited, *Hooked on the Net?*, © 2011 Bang! Science Magazine, *Getting the elderly online – improving quality of life*, © Nobilis Care Ltd, *83-year-old YouTube star leads the way online*, © Telegraph Media Group Limited 2012.

Chapter Two: Internet safety

What can go wrong?, © CEOP Child Exploitation and Online Protection Centre, *Internet safety*, © 2012 Christina Hughes, *Go online in 2012 and have fun – but think safety first*, © CEOP Child Exploitation and Online Protection Centre, *Internet safety: 'Sexting' a growing threat to children*, © 2012 MEN Media, *Self-taken images – 'sexting'*, © CEOP Child Exploitation and Online Protection Centre, *Preventing cyberbullying*, © 2012 Cyberbullying Research Center, *What is cybercrime?*, © 1995 – 2012 Symantex Corporation.

Chapter Three: Rights and privacy

Frequently asked questions about the Internet, © Speechly Bircham LLP 2010, *Online reputation*, © UK Safer Internet Centre, *Children and online privacy survey*, © Speechly Bircham LLP 2010, *SOPA and PIPA*, © 2012 Ian Stokes, *e-petition*, © Crown copyright, *Is Internet access a human right?*, © Guardian News & Media Ltd. 2012.

Illustrations

Pages 20 and 28: Don Hatcher; page 38 and 39: Angelo Madrid; pages 12 and 36: Simon Kneebone.

Images

Cover, pages i and 25: © loops7; page 8: © reekerseeker; page 10: © Marek Uliasz; page 15: © paci77; page16: © Diane Diederich; page 31: © Ed Sweetman; page 34: © Abdulhamid AlFadhly.

Additional acknowledgements

Editorial on behalf of Independence Educational Publishers by Cara Acred.
With thanks to the Independence team: Mary Chapman, Sandra Dennis, Christina Hughes, Jackie Staines and Jan Sunderland.

Cara Acred
Cambridge
September, 2012